W9-AAS-643

Organized Crime

Other Books in the Issues on Trial Series:

Organized Crime

Ronald D. Lankford, Jr., Book Editor

GREENHAVEN PRESS
A part of Gale, Cengage Learning

GALE
CENGAGE Learning™

Detroit • New York • San Francisco • New Haven, Conn • Waterville, Maine • London

GALE
CENGAGE Learning™

Christine Nasso, *Publisher*
Elizabeth Des Chenes, *Managing Editor*

© 2009 Greenhaven Press, a part of Gale, Cengage Learning

For more information, contact:
Greenhaven Press
27500 Drake Rd.
Farmington Hills, MI 48331-3535
Or you can visit our Internet site at gale.cengage.com.

For product information and technology assistance, contact us at

Gale Customer Support, 1-800-877-4253
For permission to use material from this text or product, submit all requests online at www.cengage.com/permissions

Further permissions questions can be emailed to permissionrequest@cengage.com

Articles in Greenhaven Press anthologies are often edited for length to meet page requirements. In addition, original titles of these works are changed to clearly present the main thesis and to explicitly indicate the author's opinion. Every effort is made to ensure that Greenhaven Press accurately reflects the original intent of the authors. Every effort has been made to trace the owners of copyrighted material.

Cover photograph reproduced by permission of © Bettman/CORBIS.

LIBRARY OF CONGRESS CATALOGING-IN-PUBLICATION DATA

Organized crime / Ronald D. Lankford, Jr., book editor.
      p. cm. -- (Issues on trial)
   Includes bibliographical references and index.
   ISBN-13: 978-0-7377-4180-3 (hardcover)
   1. Organized crime--United States. 2. Racketeering--United States. I. Lankford, Ronald D., 1962-
   KF9375.O74 2009
   345.73'02--dc22
                                                        2008037464

Printed in the United States of America
1 2 3 4 5 6 7 12 11 10 09 08

Contents

Chapter 1: Removing Organized Crime from Unions

Chapter 2: Organized Crime and the International Drug Trade

Chapter 3: Allowing Preventive Detention of the Accused

Chapter 4: Organized Crime Boss on Trial

Foreword

The U.S. courts have long served as a battleground for the most highly charged and contentious issues of the time. Divisive matters are often brought into the legal system by activists who feel strongly for their cause and demand an official resolution. Indeed, subjects that give rise to intense emotions or involve closely held religious or moral beliefs lay at the heart of the most polemical court rulings in history. One such case was *Brown v. Board of Education* (1954), which ended racial segregation in schools. Prior to *Brown*, the courts had held that blacks could be forced to use separate facilities as long as these facilities were equal to that of whites.

For years many groups had opposed segregation based on religious, moral, and legal grounds. Educators produced heartfelt testimony that segregated schooling greatly disadvantaged black children. They noted that in comparison to whites, blacks received a substandard education in deplorable conditions. Religious leaders such as Martin Luther King Jr. preached that the harsh treatment of blacks was immoral and unjust. Many involved in civil rights law, such as Thurgood Marshall, called for equal protection of all people under the law, as their study of the Constitution had indicated that segregation was illegal and un-American. Whatever their motivation for ending the practice, and despite the threats they received from segregationists, these ardent activists remained unwavering in their cause.

Those fighting against the integration of schools were mainly white southerners who did not believe that whites and blacks should intermingle. Blacks were subordinate to whites, they maintained, and society had to resist any attempt to break down strict color lines. Some white southerners charged that segregated schooling was *not* hindering blacks' education. For example, Virginia attorney general J. Lindsay Almond asserted, "With the help and the sympathy and the love and respect of the white people of the South, the colored man has risen under that educational process to a place of eminence and respect throughout the nation. It has served him well." So when the Supreme Court ruled against the segregationists in *Brown*, the South responded with vociferous cries of protest. Even government leaders criticized the decision. The governor of Arkansas, Orval Faubus, stated that he would not "be a party to any attempt to force acceptance of change to which the people are so overwhelmingly opposed." Indeed, resistance to integration was so great that when black students arrived at the formerly all-white Central High School in Arkansas, federal troops had to be dispatched to quell a threatening mob of protesters.

Nevertheless, the *Brown* decision was enforced, and the South integrated its schools. In this instance, the Court, while not settling the issue to everyone's satisfaction, functioned as an instrument of progress by forcing a major social change. Historian David Halberstam observes that the *Brown* ruling "deprived segregationist practices of their moral legitimacy. . . . It was therefore perhaps the single most important moment of the decade, the moment that separated the old order from the new and helped create the tumultuous era just arriving." Considered one of the most important victories for civil rights, *Brown* paved the way for challenges to racial segregation in many areas, including on public buses and in restaurants.

In examining *Brown*, it becomes apparent that the courts play an influential role—and face an arduous challenge—in shaping the debate over emotionally charged social issues. Judges must balance competing interests, keeping in mind the high stakes and intense emotions on both sides. As exemplified by *Brown*, judicial decisions often upset the status quo and initiate significant changes in society. Greenhaven Press's Issues on Trial series captures the controversy surrounding influential court rulings and explores the social ramifications of such decisions from varying perspectives. Each anthology highlights one social issue—such as the death penalty, students' rights, or wartime civil liberties. Each volume then focuses on key historical and contemporary court cases that helped mold the issue as we know it today. The books include a compendium of primary sources—court rulings, dissents, and immediate reactions to the rulings—as well as secondary sources from experts in the field, people involved in the cases, legal analysts, and other commentators opining on the implications and legacy of the chosen cases. An annotated table of contents, an in-depth introduction, and prefaces that overview each case all provide context as readers delve into the topic at hand. To help students fully probe the subject, each volume contains book and periodical bibliographies, a comprehensive index, and a list of organizations to contact. With these features, the Issues on Trial series offers a well-rounded perspective on the courts' role in framing society's thorniest, most impassioned debates.

Introduction

For many observers, the ⁕Reagan-Bush Justice Department (Ronald Reagan and George H.W. Bush; 1981–1992) successfully pursued an aggressive policy against organized crime during the 1980s and early 1990s. From the removal of organized crime's influence on labor unions in 1982 to the conviction of John Gotti in 1992, organized crime's traditional power base in New Jersey and New York had been decimated. These trials were highlighted by revelations of vast underground networks, international drug distribution, money laundering, hijacking, racketeering, and homicide.

These successes by the Justice Department had followed a lengthy history of confusion over organized crime's role in American society. Until the 1950s and 1960s, federal government officials were unclear whether organized crime—frequently referred to as the Mafia or La Cosa Nostra—even existed. Even after organized crime was identified as a societal problem, however, no one was certain how to remove its influence. Frequently, federal and state officials would bring charges against a crime family boss only to learn that a new boss had quickly taken his place and that nothing had changed.

In reaction to this stalemate, G. Robert Blakey, an attorney and law professor, helped draft legislation in the late 1960s that would become known as the Racketeer Influenced and Corrupt Organizations Act, more commonly called RICO. RICO would allow law enforcement to convict crime organizations—as opposed to individuals—by connecting multiple felonies (money laundering, drug trafficking, and larceny, for example) committed by a number of persons over a ten-year period of time. This allowed a state or federal attorney to bring charges against numerous individuals within an organized crime family in a single case. The RICO Act was passed into law in 1970, and after a lapse of ten years, became the primary law enforcement tool for fighting organized crime.

Organized Crime and the United States Constitution

For a number of critics, however, the success of the Reagan-Bush Justice Department exacted a legalistic price that negatively impacted the Bill of Rights. While the RICO legislation itself was never controversial, legal scholars questioned whether the federal courts were trimming civil liberties in the pursuit of convicting organized crime. And while there was little sympathy for organized crime figures like Anthony Salerno and Gotti, legal scholars wondered whether federal court decisions might potentially affect the civil liberties of all Americans.

In three federal trials during the 1980s and early 1990s, the clash between justice and civil rights was shown in broad relief:

- Federal Involvement in Private Organizations—One problem that law enforcement faced before the enactment of RICO was an inability to offer more than surface solutions to deeply rooted problems. In fact, in the case of *United States v. Local 560* (1984), a number of organized crime figures who had operated the union had already been convicted of a variety of crimes including fraud and murder. Incredibly, these figures continued to exert control of the Local 560 from prison through subordinates.

  In *United States v. Local 560*, the federal court radically departed from previous methods by establishing a trusteeship or governing board to oversee the activities of the Local 560. This empowered an appointed official (a trustee) or officials to promote more democratic methods within the union and to remove officials connected to organized crime. Later decisions connected with *United States v. Local 560* went so far as to remove candidates with organized crime connections from running for elective union offices.

While many of these actions undoubtedly benefited the union, the trusteeship was independent of the union. In essence, the court's decision established federal control of the Local 560 for over ten years. During that time, the Local 560 was also responsible for the costs associated with the trusteeship's decisions, including the salary of the trustee(s). The ruling in *United States v. Local 560* also seemed to leave open the possibility that the federal government could pursue similar methods in the future, though the threshold of corruption that needed to be established before the federal government became involved remained unclear.

- Pretrial Detention of Defendants—*United States v. Salerno* (1987) proved to be one of the few organized crime cases that reached the Supreme Court during the 1980s. The ruling also proved to be one of the most controversial of the era. At issue was the legality of a key provision relating to pretrial detention in the Bail Reform Act of 1984. The provision allowed courts to imprison individuals accused, but not yet convicted, of major crimes if the court believed the defendant to be a danger to the community.

Before the Bail Reform Act, the court had two methods of holding defendants: setting excessively high bail, or, in the case of capital crimes like homicide, denying bail. In effect, the Bail Reform Act would prevent the court from setting excessive bail, but expand the safeguards for defendants who were considered a threat to the community. Salerno argued that there was a basic flaw in this reasoning: In essence, the new law allowed a defendant, who had not been tried before his or her peers, to be imprisoned for an unspecified time.

The Supreme Court's ruling justified the Bail Reform Act. Chief Justice William Rehnquist ruled that pretrial detention was justifiable partly because the Fourth Amendment had never guaranteed bail, but also because Congress, in drafting the Bail Reform Act, did not intend for pretrial detention to be punishment. As long as the legal process allowed a defendant to call witnesses and present evidence against pretrial detenion, then, the Bail Reform Act of 1984 was legal.

Three justices (William J. Brennan, John Paul Stevens, and Thurgood Marshall), however, offered vigorous dissents. For these justices and civil libertarian critics, pretrial detention was the equivalent of rendering a defendant guilty before a trial had been conducted, disallowing constitutionally guaranteed due process. Furthermore, the Rehnquist ruling, they argued, failed to properly define the limits of pretrial detention, leaving open the possibility of even further misuse by future courts. By ruling such, the limits of pretrial detention would be slowly etched out in individual cases in multiple courtrooms throughout the United States for years to come.

- Legal Representation and Anonymous Juries—Two other basic rights that many Americans believed had been guaranteed by the Constitution were the freedom of a defendant to choose his or her counsel and the freedom of a defendant to be tried before his or her peers. But both of these assumptions were brought into question under unusual circumstances in *United States v. John Gotti and Frank Locascio* (1992).

Federal prosecutors argued that Gotti's counsel, Bruce Cutler, had been present during discussions of organized crime activities. Since Cutler had been present during discussions of illegal activities, it was possible that he could be called as a witness during the trial, creating a conflict of interest. Federal prosecutors also argued that Cutler's extended employment by Gotti lessened the chance that he would offer candid testimony. While this logic satisfied the federal court and the defendant's counsel was removed, it was also recognized by commentators that Cutler had successfully prevented Gotti's prosecution in previous cases. The aggressive removal of Gotti's counsel, then, proved a major benefit to the prosecution's case.

Also problematic was the anonymous jury. The reasoning behind the anonymous jury was fairly simple: In one other case involving Gotti, a juror had been bribed, an act that potentially compromised the case. It was also argued that organized crime figures could potentially threaten identified witnesses seen as "uncorporative." Gotti argued, however, that the very act of making a jury anonymous prejudiced jurors against the defendant. In a sense, he argued, making a jury anonymous was tantamount to saying, "Gotti is a dangerous organized crime figure who should be convicted."

While the trial of a well-known organized crime figure like Gotti presented special problems, removing counsel and establishing an anonymous jury were seen as forceful moves by federal prosecutors. While no one denied that Gotti had committed serious crimes, civil libertarians would once again ask difficult questions. What limits would be set on the federal court's power to remove a defendant's counsel? Was a trial by an anonymous jury equal to a trail by one's peers as guaranteed in the Constitution? As with pretrial detention, the issues surrounding these decisions would continue to reverberate in other organized crime cases in other courtrooms through the 1990s and beyond.

The Rise, Fall, and Rise of Organized Crime

Even while recognizing the ongoing conflict between justice and civil liberty issues in connection with organized crime cases, critics have agreed that the Justice Department accomplished a great deal during the 1980s and early 1990s. Through these multiple trials, the federal government removed the corrosive influence of organized crime from the Local 560, one of the biggest unions in the United States. The convictions in *United States v. Badalamenti* (1987), frequently referred to as the Pizza Connection Trial, identified and shut down a vast international drug ring. And in the lower court decision in *United States v. Salerno* (1986), the federal government conducted a massive trial that convicted multiple figures from New York City's five major crime families. By the time of Gotti's conviction in 1992, traditional Sicilian organized crime in the northeastern United States had been severely limited.

But while the RICO Act made these highly public trials possible, a number of pre-RICO problems would eventually emerge. In the past, the conviction of one crime family boss simply led to the elevation of another; now, with entire crime families weakened, new crime organizations—the Russian and Mexican Mafias, for example—filled the vacuum. Although the drug pipeline known as the Pizza Connection had been shut down by the mid-1980s, new drug suppliers quickly filled the gap. The destruction of one organized crime culture had simply allowed the elevation of others.

The emergence of new organized crime cultures calls into question the long-term effectiveness of the Justice Department's policy during the 1980s and 1990s. Meanwhile, the rulings that helped sustain the convictions and challenged traditional civil liberties continue to underpin the federal legal system in future organized crime cases. Whether these rulings continue to fall most heavily on organized crime or spill over into the general American populace remains an open question.

CHAPTER 1

Removing Organized Crime from Unions

Case Overview

United States v. Local 560 (1984)

Although the Racketeer Influenced and Corrupt Organizations Act (RICO) was passed in 1970 with the express purpose of prosecuting organized crime, there was a ten-year delay before law enforcement began using RICO as a crime-fighting tool. In the past, law enforcement had discovered that the prosecution of one organized crime figure only led to the elevation of another. The RICO legislation allowed law enforcement to make vast connections within crime organizations, tying together multiple organized crime figures (conspiracy) and legal infractions (such as racketeering), even when they had occurred over a number of years. In 1981, the United States Supreme Court sanctioned the legislation in *United States v. Turkette* (although the case itself was only nominally focused on organized crime). *United States v. Local 560* became the first federal case to seriously contest the northeastern power base of organized crime, commonly referred to as La Cosa Nostra or the Mafia.

United States v. Local 560 focused on the infiltration and control of a local teamster's union (Local 560) by organized crime, an infiltration that dated to 1961. The chief defendants were collectively known as the "Provenzano Group," a group that centered around organized crime figure Anthony Provenzano and his two bothers. This control allowed the group to profit from illegal activities conducted through the union, including overpaid contracts and the misuse of union benefit funds. The Provenzano Group also intimidated and murdered rivals. Even after a number of criminal convictions had imprisoned key members of the group (preceding this case), the Provenzano group continued to control the union through its executive board.

United States v. Local 560 stated that as long as the Provenzano Group was involved in Local 560 activities, these abuses would continue. To uproot these influences, the federal court initiated two steps. First, a number of figures who had been associated with the group would be barred from Local 560's affairs. Second, the court would appoint a governing board or trusteeship that would replace the current executive board. The trusteeship would be enjoined to remove organized crime's influence within the union and eventually foster an atmosphere where democratic elections could take place. Once these elections had taken place, the trusteeship would be dissolved.

Removing the influence of organized crime, however, proved more complicated than Judge Harold Ackerman initially believed. A number of other court decisions would be attached to *United States v. Local 560* over the next several years, most significantly *United States v. Local 560 and Michael Sciarra* (1991). Sciarra was a popular Local 560 leader, but he was considered loyal to the Provenzano Group. Although Sciarra argued that he was—in 1991—free from outside influence, evidence of wiretapped conversations revealed that organized crime figures considered him "their man." As a result, Judge Dickinson Debevoise barred Sciarra from leadership positions within Local 560.

The trusteeship created in the original *United States v. Local 560* (1984) decision and implemented following appeal (1986) remained in place until the election of Pete Brown in 1998. The following year, a congressional subcommittee listened to the testimony by Brown, trustee Edwin Stier, and others. In essence, the testimony allowed the committee to review the effectiveness of the trusteeship, and to better understand how a trusteeship might operate in future cases.

> "The associates of the Provenzano Group
> ... intended by their actions to control
> and exploit Local 560 to its detriment."

The Federal Court's Decision: Establishing the Effectiveness of RICO (Racketeer Influenced and Corrupt Organizations Act) Against Organized Crime

Harold A. Ackerman

Harold A. Ackerman was nominated to the federal circuit by President Jimmy Carter in 1979 and achieved senior status in 1994.

United States v. Local 560 *(1984) focused on the infiltration and control of one of the largest unions in the United States by organized crime. In Harold Ackerman's federal court decision, he explains that while most unions are able to operate free of organized crime control, the fate of Local 560 reveals that unions are potential targets of organized crime. In effect, he says, Anthony Provenzano and his associates infiltrated the executive body of Local 560 and used their power within the union to commit a series of crimes including racketeering. Specifically, he points to improper conduct including appointing individuals with criminal records, refusing to remove individuals who committed offenses, paying expenditures of the union to Anthony Provenzano, and systematic misconduct. To prevent these crimes from happening in the future, Ackerman barred two members of the*

Harold A. Ackerman, decision, *United States v. Local 560*, Third District, February 8, 1984. www.ipsn.org.

Provenzano Group from Local 560 activity (a number of members of the group had already been imprisoned) and formed a governing board, or trusteeship, to oversee Local 560. The implementation of these decisions, however, was stayed pending an appeal.

John L. Lewis, former president of the Congress of Industrial Organizations and the United Mine Workers once said that "Labor, like Israel, has many sorrows."

A careful review of the evidence in this unprecedented case reveals the verity of that observation.

It is not a pretty story. Beneath the relatively sterile language of a dry legal opinion is a harrowing tale of how evil men, sponsored by and part of organized criminal elements, infiltrated and ultimately captured Local 560 of the International Brotherhood of Teamsters, one of the largest local unions in the largest union in this country.

This group of gangsters, aided and abetted by their relatives and sycophants [those trying to impress to gain an advantage] engaged in a multifaceted orgy of criminal activity. For those that enthusiastically followed these arrogant mobsters in their morally debased activity, there were material rewards. For those who accepted the side benefits of this perverted interpretation of business unionism ... there was presumably the rationalization of "I've got mine, why shouldn't he get his." For those who attempted to fight, the message was clear. Murder and other forms of intimidation would be utilized to ensure silence. To get along, one had to go along, or else.

It is important to state what the evidence in this case does and does not show.

It shows that a trade union, which is by origin and nature a voluntary organization, is susceptible to the malicious machinations of others, as Congress perceived in enacting the Landrum-Griffin and RICO [Racketeer Influenced and Corrupt Organizations Act] Acts.

It does not demonstrate that unions or union officials in general are riddled with racketeering or corruption. Most authorities are convinced that the overwhelming number of unions and union officials are "untroubled by the problem of corruption."

The Provenzano Group

Since the late 1940s, Anthony Provenzano has been the leader of a group of individuals who have been associated together in fact as an illicit enterprise within the meaning of 18 U.S.C. [United States Code] § 1961(4). This group of individuals, the Provenzano Group, is presently composed of Anthony Provenzano, Nunzio Provenzano, Stephen Andretta, Thomas Andretta, Gabriel Briguglio and Andrew Reynolds, and has in the past included among its associates Salvatore Briguglio (until his murder in 1968), Salvatore Sinno (until his defection in 1961), Harold "K.O." Koningsberg (until his incarceration in the mid-1960s), Armand Faugno (until his "disappearance" in 1972), Ralph Michael Picardo (until his defection in 1975), Ralph Pellecchia (until his incarceration), and Frederick Salvatore Furino (until his murder in 1982). The Provenzano Group Enterprise did affect interstate commerce.

Continuously between approximately 1950 and the present, the aforesaid defendants, as individuals associated with the Provenzano Group Enterprise, unlawfully conducted and participated, directly or indirectly, in the conduct of that Enterprise through a pattern of racketeering activity, in continuing violation of Sections 1962(c) and 2 of Title 18 of the United States Code. The individual associates' culpability under § 1962(c) has been established by their own acts of racketeering, by their aiding and abetting the conduct of other associates, and, under *Pinkerton*, by the conduct of their co-conspirators.

Throughout this period, the defendant associates of the Provenzano Group Enterprise understood the scope of the Enterprise and had knowledge that other associates were performing tasks related to the criminal operation of the Group as such. Each had a knowing dependence upon the others for his own profit and position. The defendant associates knowingly and intentionally agreed to further the Provenzano Group Enterprise through the commission of various racketeering offenses. Therefore, I conclude that the defendant associates of the Group conspired to violate 18 U.S.C. § 1962(c), in violation of 18 U.S.C. § 1962(d). This conspiracy continues to this day.

Local 560 and its benefit funds and severance pay plan also constitute an enterprise—the Local 560 Enterprise—within the meaning of 18 U.S.C. § 1961(4), the activities of which affect interstate commerce. Continuously between approximately 1961 and the present, defendants Anthony Provenzano, Nunzio Provenzano, Salvatore Briguglio, Stephen Andretta, Thomas Andretta, Andrew Reynolds, and perhaps others, unlawfully acquired and maintained, directly and indirectly, an interest in and control of the Local 560 Enterprise through a pattern of racketeering activity, in continuing violation of Sections 1962(b) and 2 of Title 18 of the United States Code. As with the § 1962(c) violation, the culpability of the individual associates of the Provenzano Group under § 1962(b), as well as their aiders and abettors, has been established by their own conduct, by their aiding and abetting the acts of racketeering of others, and, under *Pinkerton*, by the racketeering acts of their coconspirators.

Controlling Local 560

Throughout this period, these defendants knowingly and intentionally agreed to acquire and maintain, both directly and indirectly, an interest in and control of the Local 560 Enterprise through the commission of various racketeering offenses. Each of these defendants understood the scope of this agreement and had knowledge that others were performing tasks related to the accomplishment of their purpose. Therefore, I conclude that these defendants also unlawfully conspired to violate 18 U.S.C. § 1962(b), in violation of 18 U.S.C. § 1962(d). This conspiracy also continues to this day.

Further, during their respective periods of incumbency, defendants Salvatore Provenzano, J.W. Dildine, Michael Sciarra, Stanley Jaronko, Joseph Sheridan, Josephine Provenzano and Thomas Reynolds, Sr., did aid, abet and facilitate the commission of the § 1962(b) violations. This complicity was exhibited through their appointment and retention in office of certain officials of Local 560 and in their discharge of certain other duties, the collective impact of which has, in particular, directly and substantially contributed to the existence of the climate of intimidation within the Local.

The officers of a labor organization occupy positions of trust in relation to that organization. As such, it is their duty to, among other things, hold the money and property of the labor organization on behalf of its members. Such officers should adhere to the highest standards of responsibility and ethical conduct in administering the affairs of their labor organization. Additionally, the officers have an affirmative duty and responsibility to ensure to the extent possible that the persons whom they appoint and retain in any position of trust within the labor union will adhere to the same high standards of responsibility and ethical conduct in administering the affairs of the union. In making such appointments, the incumbent union officers have an affirmative duty to ensure that they obtain the true facts with respect to the character of the potential appointee and his or her discharge of the obligations of the position. An unreasonable failure to learn the true facts as to such appointments exposes these incumbent officials to liability for such conduct. Similarly, in making such appointments, the incumbent officers have an affirmative duty to evaluate, to the greatest extent possible, the impact which any particular appointment might reasonably be expected to have on the membership in light of existing circumstances.

The Provenzano Group and Improper Conduct

Therefore, given the circumstances present within Local 560 during their respective periods of incumbency, the following conduct of the defendant officers of Local 560 was highly improper and constitutes gross misconduct:

(a) the repeated appointment of numerous individuals who had substantial criminal records (often involving crimes of violence or labor racketeering offenses) without any offsetting basis to believe that the individual would abstain from criminal conduct and meet the standards for ethical and appropriate conduct in administering the labor organization.

(b) the refusal to take any action to remove those appointees whose conduct, once in office, was clearly improper—particularly the refusal to take such action in the face of compelling circumstances such as formal allegations or proof of renewed criminal conduct, or a subsequent criminal conviction for a crime involving a direct breach of trust to the membership.

(c) the expenditure of Local 560 assets for the benefit of Anthony Provenzano who has three times committed offenses while in office, each of which constituted a direct and serious breach of trust towards the Local's membership.

(d) the reckless indifference to the persistent and systematic misconduct of fellow incumbent officers with respect to, (1) a pattern of, at best, unsuitable appointments, (2) a pattern of access to the union's offices by known or reputed criminals, and (3) a pattern of non-beneficial expenditures of Local 560 assets.

Both as gross misconduct and independently thereof, this conduct constitutes aiding and abetting of the violations of 18 U.S.C. § 1962(b). This conduct has facilitated the acquisition and maintenance, both directly and indirectly, of control of Local 560 by the Provenzano Group, most strikingly in the appointment of Group associates to officer positions, but also in contributing to the climate of fear and intimidation within the union and otherwise assisting the Provenzano Group to achieve its objectives.

The Provenzano Group, which in essence is a carefully structured and well disciplined conspiracy, has been in substantially continuous existence throughout the past thirty years, and is likely to continue. The very conditions within Local 560 which have enabled and encouraged the Provenzano Group to gain and maintain control over it and to exploit it as an instrumentality for the systematic and repeated commission of labor racketeering offenses continue in place today. Unless these conditions are changed, there is a substantial likelihood that the racketeering violations which have victimized, both the membership and the affected portions of the trucking industry will recur.

A Union Governing Board

Continuously throughout approximately the last quarter of a century, the associates of the Provenzano Group have dominated Local 560 through fear and intimidation, extorting the membership's union democracy rights, and have exploited it through fraud and corruption. Because the conditions within Local 560 [remain] ... I must conclude that future violations of 18 U.S.C. § 1962(b), (c) and (d) are likely to occur, thereby resulting in irreparable harm to the membership of Local 560, its contract employers, and the public. In order to prevent and restrain such future violations of § 1962, it is necessary to enjoin defenders Stephen Andretta and Gabriel Briguglio from any future contacts with Local 560, and to remove the current members of the Local 560 Executive Board in favor of the imposition of a trusteeship for an appropriate period of time, which will terminate following the completion of supervised elections.

I have additionally determined to exculpate [free from blame] the institutional defendants herein, specifically Local 560 itself and its Funds and Plan. In order to attribute the misconduct of the individual defendants to these institutional defendants, I must find (1) that the individual defendants committed the acts of racketeering in the scope of their employment, and (2) that they thereby intended to advance the affairs of the institutional defendants. While it is clear that the individual defendants acted within the scope of their employment in committing the various criminal acts previously recited, it is equally obvious that their intent was not to advance the affairs of their employers. To the contrary, the institutional defendants in this action were the victims. The associates of the Provenzano Group, aided and abetted by the other defendants herein intended by their actions to control and exploit Local 560 to its detriment. I, therefore, conclude that there is no basis for retaining either Local 560, the Funds or the Plan as a defendant in this action, except insofar as it is necessary to retain Local 560 as a nominal defendant to effectuate the equitable relief heretofore specified and as may be ordered in the future.

In sum, I have determined that the individual defendants herein have violated 18 U.S.C. § 1962(b), (c) and (d). Because of the likelihood of continued violations, I have determined to enjoin defendants Stephen Andretta and Gabriel Briguglio from any future contacts of any kind with Local 560, and to remove the current members of the Local 560 Executive Board in favor of a trusteeship. This trusteeship shall continue for such time as is necessary to foster the conditions under which reasonably free supervised elections can be held, presumptively for eighteen months. I have, however, decided to stay the effect of this injunctive relief pending appeal, and have also decided to defer the naming of the (trustees) until the completion of any such appellate proceedings. Finally, I have decided to dismiss Local 560, the Funds and the Plan from this action, except insofar as I must maintain jurisdiction over Local 560 as a nominal defendant in order to effectuate the equitable relief heretofore specified or as may be ordered in the future.

> *"There can be no doubt that the Gen-*
> *ovese Organized Crime Family in-*
> *tended to maintain its control over Lo-*
> *cal 560."*

The District Court's Decision: Individuals Can Be Barred from Participating in Union Elections

Dickinson Debevoise

Dickinson Debevoise was nominated to the federal circuit by President Jimmy Carter in 1978 and achieved senior status in 1994.

The establishment of a trusteeship, or federal governing body, in United States v. Local 560 (1984) was only the beginning of an ongoing attempt by federal authorities to remove the influence of organized crime from the union. One ongoing issue was the presence of Michael Sciarra within the union leadership. The federal government argued that Sciarra had close ties to organized crime and should be barred from holding union office; Sciarra argued that he had severed his ties with organized crime and that barring him from union office violated his civil rights. Throughout the late 1980s, the court was unable to decisively settle the issue, eventually leading to Sciarra's return to union leadership. His elevation as de facto *leader prompted the court to review evidence against him once again. Judge Dickinson Debevoise relates that a series of wiretapped conversations of orga-*

Dickinson Debevoise, decision, *United States v. Local 560 and Michael Sciarra*, Third District, January 7, 1991. www.thelaborers.net.

nized crime figures revealed that Sciarra continued to work closely with organized crime, basically serving as someone who would carry out organized crime's instructions within the union. Because of the evidence proving the connection, the court barred Sciarra from all involvement within the leadership of Local 560.

In this proceeding the government seeks a permanent injunction against Michael Sciarra prohibiting him from further participation in the affairs of Local 560. The trial was conducted on July 16, 1990, but only two witnesses were presented, and the bulk of the evidence upon which a decision must be based was introduced upon applications for preliminary injunctive relief. This opinion constitutes my findings of fact and conclusions of law.

Barring Organized Crime from Local 560

This case is an outgrowth of and now a part of, an action which the government commenced on March 9, 1982 pursuant to the Racketeer Influenced and Corrupt Organizations Act ("RICO Act"). Asserting that Local 560 of the International Brotherhood of Teamsters was being victimized by racketeering activity, the complaint sought injunctive relief against individual defendants Anthony Provenzano, Nunzio Provenzano, Thomas Andretta, Stephen Andretta and Gabriel Briguglio, as associates of the so-called "Provenzano Group." The complaint also sought injunctive relief against the Local 560 Executive Board incumbents, Salvatore Provenzano, Joseph Sheridan, Josephine Provenzano, J.W. Dildine, Thomas Reynolds Sr., Michael Sciarra and Stanley Jaronko.

On February 8, 1984, after lengthy hearings, the Honorable Harold A. Ackerman issued an opinion, holding that the Provenzano Group, through racketeering activity, had dominated and exploited Local 560 for more than a quarter of a century. Judge Ackerman issued a Judgment Order on March 16, 1984 in which the court: (a) enjoined Stephen Andretta and Gabriel Briguglio from having any future dealings with and from endeavoring to influence the affairs of Local 560 or any other labor organization or employee benefit plan; (b) removed from office temporarily the remaining incumbent Executive Board members (including Sciarra); and (c) imposed a trusteeship upon Local 560 for such period of time as might be necessary to eliminate the racketeer influence within Local 560 and to restore democratic processes within the Union. Prior to trial, Anthony Provenzano, Nunzio Provenzano and Thomas Andretta entered into consent decrees barring them forever from participating in, or otherwise interfering with, the affairs of Local 560 or any other "labor organization" or "employee benefit plan."

Judge Ackerman stayed his March 16, 1984 Judgment Order pending appeal. In consequence, Sciarra and the other members of the Executive Board of Local 560 remained in office.

On December 26, 1985, the Court of Appeals for the Third Circuit affirmed the judgment of the district court, and on May 27, 1986 the Supreme Court denied a petition for certiorari [review]. On June 23, 1986, Judge Ackerman lifted the stay and implemented the Trusteeship provided for in the Judgment Order. Thus, there was a period of approximately two years, four and one-half months between Judge Ackerman's February 1984 opinion detailing the racketeering activity and the 1986 appointment of the trustee and ouster of the Executive Board. During that period, on October 19, 1984 to be precise, Sciarra succeeded Salvatore Provenzano (who had been convicted of defrauding the welfare benefit fund and of receiving kickbacks) as President of Local 560. What transpired during that period is one of the principal subjects of the present proceeding.

Appointing Trustees and Union Elections

Judge Ackerman appointed Joel Jacobson Trustee of Local 560 on June 23, 1986. On May 12, 1987, Judge Ackerman appointed Edwin H. Stier, Esq., in place of Jacobson, and he appointed as Associate Trustee Frank Jackiewicz. Stier undertook numerous measures to achieve his three principal objectives: (a) conducting the day-to-day operations of the union so as to provide effective representation to the membership, (b) using his own background in conducting investigations to organize and oversee inquiries into the affairs of the union and of the pension and welfare funds, and (c) encouraging the members of Local 560 to throw off years of passivity in the face of Provenzano domination and to participate in the affairs of the union.

In early 1988 Stier concluded that although the forces conducive to an uncoerced atmosphere within Local 560 were still fragile and still threatened with organized crime efforts to regain control, an election with suitable controls was feasible.

On February 11, 1988, Judge Ackerman extended the Trusteeship until December 6, 1988 and ordered that general elections be held prior to that date. Nominations were to be made at a membership meeting called for October 9, 1988, and the election by secret ballot was scheduled for November, ballots to be mailed to each member's home to reduce the opportunities for undue pressure.

Certain developments came to the attention of the government which led it to believe that unless injunctive relief were obtained, the result of the election would be to return Local 560 to the control of organized crime, specifically the Genovese Family. The strongest faction competing for control of Local 560 was Teamsters for Liberty, a group which had never evidenced a critical view of the former leadership and which was dedicated to termination of the Trusteeship. That stance of itself was no reason to interfere with the efforts of Teamsters for Liberty. However, the government had come into possession of evidence which led it to believe that the Genovese Family had determined to regain control of Local 560 and that it had designated Michael Sciarra as the Person through whom it would exercise control. Sciarra was a dominant force in Teamsters for Liberty, and he and Joseph Sheridan, also a former Executive Board member when the Provenzano Group was in control, were Teamsters for Liberty's candidates for President and Vice-President, respectively.

Faced with that situation and with the fragile nature of Local 560's democratic forces, the government instituted the present proceedings, seeking an order prohibiting Sciarra and Sheridan from further participation in the affairs of Local 560.

The Federal Government v. Michael Sciarra

The government filed an Application for Additional Relief and obtained an order to show cause in the original Local 560 case. Sciarra and Sheridan raised a procedural barrier, namely that they were no longer parties to the original action and that therefore relief could not be sought against them by way of order to show cause. In light of this procedural question the government served upon Sciarra and Sheridan a complaint embodying the same allegations and requests for relief as were contained in the order to show cause application.

I treated the government's application as a request to amend or supplement the complaint pursuant to Fed.R.Civ.P. 15(a) and (b). The relief requested was an order preliminarily enjoining Sciarra and Sheridan from any further participation in and from otherwise endeavoring to influence the affairs of Local 560. By way of ultimate relief the government sought a permanent injunction containing the same prohibition.

On September 14, 1988, after a six-day hearing, I granted preliminary injunctive relief, barring Sciarra and Sheridan from seeking elective office. Teamsters for Liberty substituted as its candidates for President and Vice-President Sciarra's brother Daniel Sciarra and Sheridan's nephew Mark Sheridan.

The election was carefully monitored and fairly conducted, and on December 6, 1988, it was announced that the Teamsters for Liberty slate had won. As a result Daniel Sciarra and

Mark Sheridan assumed the offices for which they ran. Other Teamsters for Liberty candidates had been elected to complete the Executive Board. Stier, the Trustee, turned over the day-to-day administration of Local 560 to the newly elected officers and Executive Board but continued to serve in a monitoring role.

The Continued Influence of Michael Sciarra

On January 9, 1989, the newly elected Board appointed both Michael Sciarra and Joseph Sheridan to fill business agent positions. Thereupon the government obtained an order to show cause why they should not be immediately barred from holding any appointed position within Local 560 pending the outcome of the trial in the matter. The government urged that Sciarra and Sheridan gave the appearance of acting as *de facto* officers of the Local and of exercising actual power consistent with that of incumbent Executive Board members, thus creating the risk of reemergence of Genovese Family control of the Union.

At a hearing on January 30, 1989, I concluded that the development was troubling but that I should not assume without more that the new officers and Executive Board would not exercise full control of the Union or that they would be subject to Sciarra's domination and influence. Consequently I denied the government's application at that time.

The Trustee [Stier] . . . continued to monitor closely the management of the Union. The new officers and Executive Board members entered upon their duties. Subsequently, Sheridan entered into a settlement with the government, resigning as business agent and agreeing not to involve himself in the future in the management of Local 560. Michael Sciarra, however, remained highly involved in the Union's affairs.

On February 6, 1990, the government moved once again to bar Sciarra from holding any position of trust in the Union, asserting that evidence relating to events during the previous thirteen months showed that Sciarra had used his hold on a large and vocal segment of the Local 560 membership and his position as business agent to acquire control of the Union. A second preliminary injunction hearing was held on March 20 and 21, and I concluded that Sciarra had indeed become virtually *de facto* President of Local 560. On May 8, 1990, I signed an order preliminarily enjoining Sciarra from holding any position of trust within Local 560 and from attempting to influence its affairs.

I scheduled a trial on an expedited basis. The trial began on July 16, 1990. Relying upon the entire prior record in the litigation, the government presented one additional witness. Prior to the trial, Sciarra submitted a list of approximately seventy witnesses he expected to call at trial. However, when the time came, only he testified. Thus, this matter must be decided upon the facts established at the trial before Judge Ackerman as set forth in his February 8, 1984 opinion and upon the additional evidence presented at the two preliminary injunction hearings and at the trial of the amended and supplemental complaint which seeks relief against Sciarra. . . .

Evidence Against Sciarra

The totality of the evidence establishes that: (i) Since March 16, 1984, when Judge Ackerman signed the order granting relief, the Genovese Family has sought to maintain or reestablish its control over Local 560; (ii) Michael Sciarra was the person through whom the Genovese Family sought to effectuate its control; (iii) Sciarra accepted this role; (iv) Sciarra has a dominating and forceful personality, and there are no leaders or factions within Local 560 who are able to resist him and the forces within the Union which he controls; and (v) unless Sciarra is removed from any position within Local 560 he will assume control of the Union, directly or indirectly, and thereby subjugate Local 560 once again to the control of the Genovese Organized Crime Family.

The continuing determination of the Genovese Family to maintain control of Local 560 is evidenced by the tape recordings of three conversations held in a construction shed in Edgewater, New Jersey, and by one tape recording of a conversation held at the Palma Boy Social Club in East Harlem. When viewed in conjunction with the findings in *Local 560*, they demonstrate that the efforts of this organized crime group to control Local 560 did not cease with the entry of Judge Ackerman's order. . . .

The First Conversation. The first conversation took place on November 1, 1984, and involved Milton Parness, Matthew Ianniello (a captain in the Genovese Family), Stanley Jaronko (who served on Local 560's Executive Board with Sciarra), and an unidentified male. Ianniello and Jaronko discussed continued control of Local 560. Jaronko stated that he would "just lay low for eighteen months" (the period during which it was expected a court-appointed trustee would be in office). It was in that conversation that Ianniello directed Jaronko to "let Mike run the show." The reference was to "Mikey Sciarra."

The Second Conversation. The second tape records a November 6, 1984 conversation between Ianniello and Stephen Andretta (one of the defendants who was a member of the Provenzano Group). It was a lengthy conversation concerning numerous persons in the Genovese Family, past and pending criminal endeavors, and the Local 560 RICO case. As to the situation at Local 560, Ianniello stated, "I think Mike Sciarra should take over there. Who can you trust there, anybody else?" Andretta responded, "Mike and I were born and raised together." Later Ianniello stated, "I'll send word to [Mike]. I'll make sure that he knows that you can talk to him as one." There followed this interchange:

Ianniello: No, no, I'll send word to Mike (unintelligible).

Andretta: I can see Mike any time you want me to.

Ianniello: You?

Andretta: Yeah.

The Third Conversation. The third tape records a December 7, 1984 conversation between Ianniello, Stephen Andretta, and an unidentified male. That too was a lengthy conversation which dealt with a number of subjects of significance in this case, one of the more important subjects being the New England Motor Freight ("NEMF") contract. As to the role which Sciarra was to play, the following is illustrative:

Andretta: I understand at this point. But with Mikey and then you, you have direct control of Mikey.

Ianniello: Yeah.

Andretta: No question.

Ianniello: Yeah, he does what I tell him.

The Fourth Conversation. A fourth tape recorded conversation had taken place on November 28, 1984 in the Palma Boy Social Club in New York City. The participants were then Genovese Family boss Anthony Salerno, Louis Gatto, one of his caporegimes, Giuseppe Sabato and Cirino Salerno. The conversation turned to Local 560, and the following exchange took place:

A. Salerno: But they threw everybody out of office there.

Sabato: Yeah, they're all out.

A. Salerno: Everybody's out.

Sabato: They're all out.

A. Salerno: So how can you control it?

Sabato: What do you mean? They got the control in there.

A. Salerno: Who is that now?

Sabato: Matty (Ianniello).

A. Salerno: Oh, we got a guy in there?

Sabato: Sure.

The Sciarra—Organized Crime Connection. These taped conversations must be viewed in the light of the facts disclosed in the 1984 *Local 560*. . . . When so viewed there can be no doubt that the Genovese Organized Crime Family intended to maintain its control over Local 560 during the pendency of the appeal from Judge Ackerman's March 16, 1984 Judgment Order, during any period of trusteeship and thereafter. I concluded after the first preliminary injunction hearing and I conclude now that the tapes constitute strong evidence that this control was to be exercised through Anthony Salerno's caporegime Matthew Ianniello and that Ianniello, upon the advice of Stephen Andretta, selected Michael Sciarra to be the man on the scene at Local 560 to whom orders and instructions could be given.

Thus, notwithstanding the issuance of the March 16, 1984 Judgment Order and the appointment of a trustee on June 23, 1986, the Provenzano Group as it existed in 1984 and as its personnel changed somewhat during the years that followed, never ceased the unlawful conduct described in Judge Ackerman's opinion in *Local 560*. . . .

Barring Sciarra from Local 560

I have concluded that additional relief is necessary to prevent irreparable injury to the Union, its members and the Union's pension and welfare funds. The additional relief required is a permanent injunction prohibiting Sciarra from holding any position of trust within or otherwise endeavoring to influence the affairs of Local 560 or any of its benefit plans.

Sciarra urges that a permanent injunction would deny him his Fifth Amendment rights to liberty and property by preventing him from pursuing his means of livelihood as an officer, Executive Board member or business agent of Local 560. Throughout his adult life, Sciarra has been a member or employee of Local 560, from which he has derived his income and upon which he and his family have depended for a livelihood and support. . . .

Although the Third Circuit addressed an order which only temporarily removed the Executive Board members from office, the language and the logic of its opinion would permit a district court to enjoin a defendant such as Sciarra from reacquiring union office. The statute permits such relief and there is no constitutional impediment to granting such relief.

The only question, therefore, is whether a permanent injunction against Sciarra is a *reasonable* restriction . . . I have concluded that it is both reasonable and necessary.

It is necessary for the reasons I have elaborated in my factual findings. It is reasonable that the injunction be permanent rather than remaining in effect for only a designated number of years.

Sciarra has opportunities for work other than employment as an officer, Executive Board member or business agent of Local 560. He is at that stage in life where he has acquired pension interests based upon his employment by Local 560. The preliminary injunction decree issued after the second preliminary injunction hearing was tailored so as to enable him to become eligible for payment of pension benefits. Thus, any hardship upon Sciarra and his family has been minimized.

Sciarra also argues that a lesser remedy should be decreed, namely an order which would permit him to continue as a business agent and which would impose tight restrictions on what he could and could not do. That suggestion has some appeal. However, we have already tried that approach and, as described above, it was a dismal failure. . . .

For all the foregoing reasons, I conclude that additional relief is required. An order will be entered permanently enjoining Michael Sciarra from holding any office or position of trust within or otherwise endeavoring to influence the affairs of Local 560 or any of its benefit plans. The government is requested to submit a form of order.

> *"The successful use of civil RICO against IBT [International Brotherhood of Teamsters] Local 560 demonstrated a new and powerful weapon against labor racketeering."*

Trusteeships Can Be Powerful Weapons Against Crime

James B. Jacobs

James B. Jacobs is a legal scholar and law professor at New York University of Law.

In the following excerpt, James B. Jacobs asserts that United States v. Local 560 *(1984) was significant for several reasons. First, he says, the ruling went beyond previous rulings involving organized crime and union activity by creating a governing board or trusteeship. The trusteeship gave the federal government the power to continually oversee the union's activities until the influence of organized crime was removed. The oversight of the trusteeship was eventually assigned to Edwin Stier who had extensive experience in crime fighting. Working with union members, Stier was able to purge individuals connected with organized crime and encourage union members to embrace leadership positions. He also maintains that it was helpful that a federal court eventually barred the influential Michael Sciarra from running for union office because of his connections to organized crime. According to Jacobs, although it took Stier ten years to complete his work, the success of his work revealed that a trust-*

James B. Jacobs, *Mobsters, Unions and Feds: The Mafia and the American Labor Movement*, New York, NY: New York University Press, 2006, pp. 178–182. Copyright *eeship could offer a powerful weapon against organized crime when traditional methods failed to work.*

A lengthy trial enabled Judge [Harold] Ackerman to learn firsthand the depth of the corruption and racketeering in Local 560, which he branded a "multifaceted orgy of criminal activity." Over the course of the fifty-one-day bench trial, witnesses detailed organized crime's entrenchment in IBT [International Brotherhood of Teamsters] Local 560. Ackerman heard Genovese capo (and the government's star witness) Salvatore Sinno testify about the link between the union and Genovese crime family. He listened to Executive Board members express admiration for Tony Provenzano, a convicted murderer, labor racketeer, and organized crime member. Such testimony persuaded Ackerman to impose a heretofore unprecedented remedy, a court-appointed trustee empowered with all the authority of the union's Executive Board. It should not be forgotten that Ackerman himself had been a union lawyer before being appointed to the bench and was thus almost uniquely qualified to understand the "situation on the ground" that needed to be changed. Furthermore, Ackerman had considerable experience in a prior institutional reform case involving the Essex County jail.

Most all civil RICO [Racketeer Influenced and Corrupt Organizations Act] actions against mobbed-up unions have been resolved by negotiated consent decrees. In such cases, the judge who approves the decree may not fully grasp the magnitude of the corruption and not have become personally committed to ending it. Without a trial, the government may have negotiated a settlement with Local 560 that was not as far-reaching as Judge Ackerman's order. Furthermore, because of the trial, Ackerman was in a position to deal confidently with subsequent DOJ [Department of Justice] motions. At every step of the way, [Edwin] Stier [the Trustee] benefited from the strong support of the federal Organized Crime Strike Force, especially Assistant U.S. Attorney Robert Stewart, who stayed with the case from beginning to end. Judge Ackerman's and Judge [Dickinson] Debevoise's determination were also critical.

Judge Ackerman defined the trustee's goal in broad and ambitious terms. He empowered the trustee "to act as he may, in good judgment, to administer the affairs of Local 560 and to create and foster conditions under which union democracy will be restored and racketeer influence will be eliminated." The remedial decree authorized the trustee to implement whatever policies he deemed necessary and in the best interest of the local. Unlike trustees in other civil RICO consent decrees, Stier was not burdened with the time-consuming process of repeatedly having to petition the court for approval prior to instituting reforms.

Transforming the Role of the Trustee

Although Ackerman applauded the efforts of his first trustee, Joel Jacobson, he knew that a different approach was needed to "insure that the documented egregious pattern of racketeering activity does not re-emerge. . . ." Jacobson had extensive experience in union governance, but not in combating organized crime. Clearly, investigative and prosecutorial expertise was needed. When Ackerman appointed Edwin Stier and Frank Jackiewicz, he wrote that the two men "bring to the task at hand unique talents which in combination are essential for this new phase of the trusteeship." With Stier's appointment, Ackerman in effect redefined the trustee's primary job as purging organized crime.

Stier's prosecutorial background turned out to be critically important. He worked easily and effectively with FBI and DOL [Department of Labor] investigators and with federal prosecutors. Still, it may also have been important that Stier did not fully delegate his union administrative powers to Jackiewicz, believing it necessary to participate personally in Local 560's affairs, including collective bargaining, strikes, and picketing, in order to understand the organization and culture of the local, and to establish credibility with the rank-and-file membership. It is certainly important that Stier was able to devote practically all his time to the trusteeship for several years. At the time he took the job, he operated like a full-time consultant rather than like a big-law-firm partner whose duties as a trustee may be just one of many professional responsibilities.

Development of New Union Leaders

To succeed in reforming IBT Local 560, Trustee Stier needed to recruit and develop a new cadre of union leaders. It was a major challenge because, for decades, the only members with leadership experience were either members or supporters of the Provenzano Group.

From the outset, Stier sought to create an atmosphere conducive to the emergence of new leaders. He appointed several members to the contract-negotiating committees, a role once reserved for Tony Provenzano's henchmen. As new people began to assume official responsibilities, Stier steadily delegated more administrative responsibilities. He did not offer training programs for emerging leaders because he feared that the membership would view participants as government pawns. In distancing himself from the local's government, Stier helped to legitimize the board as an independent body.

Union members who had not held office before gained experience as shop stewards and Executive Board members. As time passed, these leaders gained the respect of the general membership. The 1998 election of Peter Brown illustrated this shift. Brown, who had been vilified for his protrustee stance in the 1980s, soundly defeated his opponents in the 1998 election and was easily reelected in 2001 and 2004.

Purging Organized Crime

Stier's dogged effort to purge organized crime's influence from Local 560 was essential to the reform project. Stier had to excise every vestige of the Provenzano/Sciarra regime. If union members thought there was any chance of organized crime regaining control of the union, they would not support the reform effort. Stier realized the paramount importance of eliminating the Genovese crime family's handpicked successor, Michael Sciarra, and his successor, Daniel Sciarra, from Local 560.

DOJ's assistance was essential for Stier's success. When Stier sought judicial intervention, he was steadfastly supported by Assistant U.S. Attorney Robert Stewart, who had drafted the RICO complaint and tried the case against the Local 560 officers. Stewart drafted virtually all of the government's motions relating to Local 560. Few government attorneys involved in union RICO cases have had Stewart's longevity. His knowledge of the multiple challenges faced by the trusteeship allowed him to respond effectively to Stier's concerns. Stewart and Stier acquired enough evidence to prove that the Genovese crime family had designated Michael Sciarra as boss of the local. Judge Debevoise enjoined Michael Sciarra and Joseph Sheridan from running for office. Later, Sciarra was expelled from the union.

Two federal judges played critical roles in eradicating organized crime from the union. Judge Harold Ackerman realized the extent of organized crime's entrenchment in the union and resisted the temptation to bow to the local's initial desire for self-regulation. He did not back off in the face of the TFL's [Teamsters for Liberty] rallies or characterization of the civil RICO as antiunion.

Judge Debevoise's decision to grant an injunction to forbid Michael Sciarra from running for Local 560 office came at a crucial moment. Although Michael Sciarra still exerted influence after his brother Daniel was elected president, had Michael been elected by the membership, the Provenzano Group's power would have been legitimated.

Reforming a Union

Civil RICO provided a means for achieving reforms, but successfully reforming a racketeer-ridden union like Local 560 requires significant time. By serving for *ten years*, Trustee Stier provided constant pressure for reform. No other trustee in any labor racketeering case has served that long. The trustee's longevity symbolized to the rank and file the court's determination to reform the union; it also provided the trustee with invaluable knowledge and experience. Prosecutors and judges may wish for a quick fix in such cases, but the history of the IBT [International Brotherhood of Teamsters] Local 560 case indicates that the trustee's own determination is an important factor. As time passed, Local 560's membership changed. Through the natural process of relocation and retirement, many Local 560 members who had lived under the Provenzano Group's reign were succeeded by workers who had not experienced [La] Cosa Nostra's domination and had never met or seen the Provenzanos.

Stier assigned high priority to the protection of the pension and welfare funds. One of his first acts as trustee was to appoint himself the funds' sole trustee. He ordered a background check on all companies and individuals that provided services to the funds. Stier made Local 560's funds the first in the country to be invested solely in index funds, so that an active fund manager was not required. To further ensure the integrity of the funds, Stier hired Deloitte & Touche to perform regular audits, which were made available to the membership. Stier also hired a full-time controller to serve as chief financial officer. The pension and welfare funds' performance improved markedly, producing increased member benefits. This achievement boosted Stier's credibility and popularity.

A Powerful Weapon Against Organized Crime

Although, prior to the government's 1982 civil RICO suit, sporadic criminal prosecutions sent Tony Provenzano, his brothers, and several associates to prison, the prosecutions did not loosen the racketeers' grip on the union. Remarkably, the indictments and convictions did not break, or perhaps even weaken, the Provenzanos' control over Local 560.

The failure of past criminal prosecutions led the Newark federal Organized Crime Strike Force to initiate the first-ever civil RICO action against a labor organization. Replacing the Executive Board with a court-appointed trustee paved the way for purging LCN [La Cosa Nostra] and ultimately returning the local to its members. Judge Ackerman and Trustee Stier succeeded because of a confluence of factors, some well planned and executed, others merely fortuitous. Judge Ackerman's novel decree focused not only on the need to run the union honestly but also on the need to purge LCN's influence. His wide-ranging decree paved the way for Stier to reform the local. Stier's skill in developing a new cadre of union leaders eventually led to the reconstruction of the union and to significant numbers of members recognizing that the new union was far better than the old. . . . One could not have anticipated the determination and perseverance of Judge Ackerman, Trustee Stier, and Assistant U.S. Attorney Stewart. Yet . . . seems likely that the trusteeship would not have been successful without their sustained commitment. Ultimately, Stier succeeded because of two interrelated strategies. He and Stewart kept continuous pressure on the Provenzano Group, purging its members from the union. Stier identified, encouraged, and supported future leaders from the local's rank and file.

The successful use of civil RICO against IBT Local 560 demonstrated a new and powerful weapon against labor racketeering. After *United States v. Local 560*, the Justice Department brought similar suits against many other racketeer-ridden unions. However, victory at the trial and the imposition of a trusteeship are only necessary preconditions for success; they do not guarantee success.

> "The strategies that you develop as a trustee must be strategies that include the membership."

Lessons Learned from the Local 560 Trusteeship

Pete Hoekstra, Edwin Stier, and Pete Brown

Representative Pete Hoekstra has served as a member of Congress from Michigan since 1993. Edwin Stier served as the court-appointed trustee of Local 560 for ten years. Pete Brown was elected president of Local 560 in 1998.

When a federal court created a trusteeship to oversee the Local 560 in 1984, no one imagined that it would take the governing body fourteen years to eliminate the influence of organized crime from the union. Reporting to Congress, Edwin Stier, who served as the primary trustee of the union for over ten years, reviews the accomplishments of the trusteeship. While many considered the appointment of the trusteeship an extreme measure, Stier maintains that it was a necessary step: Traditional methods of law enforcement had failed to remove the influence of organized crime in Local 560 union activity. He points out that the trusteeship allowed him to reform union culture within Local 560 and set standards of conduct for its members. The current president of Local 560, Pete Brown, adds to these comments that the trusteeship was successful because the right person—Stier—had been chosen to operate it. But while the trusteeship had been a neces-

Pete Hoekstra, Edwin Stier, and Pete Brown, "Lessons Learned from the Teamsters Local 560 Trusteeship Hearing," Subcommittee on Oversight and Investigations of the Committee on Education and the Workforce, 106th Congress, First Session, June 30, 1999. http://commdocs.house.gov.

sary step in removing the influence of organized crime, Brown emphasizes that the federal government should have no permanent place in union activity.

*C*hairman Pete Hoekstra: The subcommittee will come to order. Today we are here to take a look at a case study.

Teamsters Local 560 in Union City, New Jersey, was at one time a symbol of the power and arrogance that organized crime had achieved in this country. For more than 30 years, Local 560 was dominated by the notorious Provenzano family. The Provenzanos, who were linked to the Genovese crime family, used Local 560 to carry out a full range of criminal activities including murder, extortion, loan sharking, kickbacks, highjacking, and gambling.

In 1982, the U.S. Department of Justice in a novel attempt to clean up Local 560 filed a civil RICO [Racketeer Influenced and Corrupt Organizations Act] lawsuit against 12 individuals. This lawsuit was the first of its kind against the union. The government alleged that these individuals had violated the RICO statute by engaging in a pattern of racketeering activity which included murder, numerous acts of extortion, and labor racketeering. After a lengthy court trial and exhaustion of all appeals, Local 560 was placed into a trusteeship on June 23, 1986.

More than 13 years ago. That is a long time.

Ending the Trusteeship

On February 25, 1999, after nearly 13 years of close government oversight, a Federal judge in New Jersey ended the trusteeship of Local 560 and returned the union to its members. When the court first imposed this trusteeship back in 1986, no one envisioned that it would take more than a decade to eliminate racketeering and restore the democratic process to the local.

The job proved to be a major challenge and required an evolution of change in the entire culture of the union. We are

51

very fortunate here today to have a panel of witnesses with in-depth knowledge of the Local 560 trusteeship. The subcommittee is looking forward to learning more about local 560's efforts to clean up their union; specifically, what worked, what didn't work, and what criteria was used to determine that the trusteeship should be lifted. This information will be helpful as the subcommittee continues to monitor the International Brotherhood of Teamsters. . . .

Mr. [Edwin] Stier: Thank you, Mr. Chairman and members of the committee. I am honored to be here. I am honored to be here on my own behalf. It is always, I think, inspiring to come into the halls of Congress and be asked to testify and provide information to committee. I am also honored, on behalf of the people that I have worked with for 15 years at Local 560 because it is the people of Local 560, the members of Local 560, who deserve the real credit for the successful completion of this trusteeship. My job was to facilitate a process by which the membership could achieve that success. What I would like to do is to spend just a couple of minutes outlining some of the major principles that, I think, can be derived for trusteeships from the experience that I had at Local 560. . . .

The Purpose of a RICO Trusteeship

There are several important lessons to be learned, I think, from the experience that I had at Local 560. Let me start out with the first of those lessons, which is that we need to recognize that a RICO trusteeship is an extremely heavy burden. It is an extremely powerful weapon, and it should be used only under the most limited circumstances to achieve very specific objectives. That is that the whole notion of a RICO enterprise is that an institution that is important to society has been literally taken over by racketeers and is being run by them for their benefit and represents a threat to the general public because of the fact that it is controlled, dominated, and abused by racketeers.

Looking at the flip side of that idea, the processes, the internal controls that we typically rely on in our important social institutions to prevent racketeer exploitation simply don't work anymore in that case. And so we can't rely on the institution to protect the public from its misuse by racketeers. We don't impose a trusteeship because corruption has occurred. We use the criminal process, we conduct criminal investigations and prosecute people when we believe that corruption has occurred. We use a RICO trusteeship when we believe that the institution itself has been corrupted so that racketeering becomes self-generating.

Therefore, the goal is not to punish individual conduct, not simply to take over so that we can remove bad guys from the union. The purpose of the trusteeship is to reform the institution itself so that the institution becomes self-correcting so that the institution can then purge itself of any remaining corruption. I think it is really very important when you go into this sort of enterprise, that is, as a trustee, that the objective be defined very, very carefully, and that measures of success or failure be defined very carefully so that you remain focused on the objective of helping the institution itself. In this case, help a union reestablish the capacity to protect itself and the public from racketeer exploitation.

Reforming Union Culture

The second point that I want to make is that the role of a trustee, particularly somebody with my background, as you may know from the information that you have received, I did not come to this job because I had experience as a labor leader. I was appointed by Judge Ackerman, because of my experience as a law enforcement official.

I had spent 17 years investigating and prosecuting organized crime in New Jersey, at the Federal and State levels, and Judge Ackerman believed at that stage, and I was the second trustee, the first was in place for 10 months, that he needed somebody who would be more knowledgeable about and confrontational with organized crime.

It is a very difficult role. Your job is not to identify and remove criminals. Your job to help the union reform its culture, which is a very different kind of role for a former prosecutor.

You can't impose that change on the union, as a trustee. It must come from the membership itself. So, the strategies that you develop as a trustee must be strategies that include the membership. You must be prepared to participate in an honest, open, and forthright way with the membership in helping to reform the union.

To a certain extent your role is self-defeating. The more active you are as a trustee, the more it costs the union. They are paying for your time and the more you run the risk of stigmatizing those who cooperate with you and support you as government supporters, government advocates, government agents, which in the context of a union, even the most honest union, can hurt union members politically. You have got to be very careful to strike a balance between imposing high costs and stigmatizing the people that you need for support to help the membership reform itself.

In the process, you have to develop an understanding for trade union values and the trade union perspective. You can't set expectations that are based on your point of view as a prosecutor. You have got to look at the world through the eyes of somebody who is a member of a labor union and depends on that labor union for their livelihood and for protecting their livelihood.

The other side of your responsibilities involves dealing with the government, the Department of Justice, the FBI, and the Department of Labor, who are not always on the same schedule you are and don't always see things the way that you do. So, the trustee can become somewhat caught in the middle. It is up to the trustee to maintain credibility on both sides with the government and with the union.

Defining Standards of Conduct

The third point that I want to make is that, as the trustee, you have got to help the membership develop the capacity to reform the culture of the union by defining standards of conduct, goals that are clear, reasonable, and attainable. That is, the membership needs to know what it has to do in order to bring about an end to the trusteeship.

Those goals and objectives need to be defined in terms that the membership can understand, are realistic, and that become part of their culture, part of their value system; not simply goals that are hoops that they have to jump through in order to get rid of the government. They have to truly believe that what you are trying to achieve with them has a value to the union itself. I spent a lot of time working with the elected officials of the union to assure them that they were going to be judged on the basis of fair and objective standards. In some cases, particularly early in the trusteeship, I was dealing with people who had very close associations with the Provenzano group. My position was that as long as you are not barred from holding office in this union, I am going to treat you as somebody who could remain in this job after the trusteeship is over, unless you violate standards of conduct that all of us agree should control the conduct of a union official.

Basically, the standards that I set were quite simple. You have got to protect the assets and resources of the union, that is, you can't steal from the union or the pension and welfare funds. You have got to represent everybody in the union in an evenhanded way, not taking care of your friends and hurting your enemies, but representing everybody in a way that protects their interests as union members.

Each member of the executive board, each official has his own individual fiduciary responsibility to assure that every other official of that union is behaving in a responsible way. One of the most important provisions of Judge Ackerman's opinion had to do not with the Provenzanos and the others who were guilty of various crimes, including extortion and murder, but with those who sat back and facilitated what they did by failing to respond when it was clear that crimes were being committed that victimized the members and the general public.

Developing an Open Dialogue

The final point that I want to make is that to achieve the successful conclusion of this trusteeship, I had to work very closely with and establish a very open dialogue with the leadership of Local 560, all of the leadership of Local 560. I had to understand how they thought, and they had to understand how I thought. As we worked together over time and as it became clear what my expectations were, more importantly, that those expectations were the same expectations that a leader of any union should have for the way in which leadership should conduct itself, we began to work for the same goal.

That same goal was to bring an end to the trusteeship. That has been my objective from day one. It took 12 years, but frankly, I wish that it had occurred even sooner. My job was to work myself out of a position. As I said over and over again to every leader of Local 560 from the day that I set foot in the union hall, no trusteeship can ever be viewed as successful until it is brought to an end.

That concludes my remarks. . . .

Mr. Pete Brown: Good afternoon. My name is Pete Brown. I have been a teamster for 30 years and a member of Local 560 for more than 20 years. I have been through the trusteeship from the beginning to the end. I am currently the president and principal officer of Local 560.

First, I would like to thank you, Chairman Hoekstra and the other members of the committee for the opportunity to testify about the trusteeship, both for myself and for the members of Local 560. It has been a long and sometimes painful process, but I think that we have learned from it. I think some valuable and extremely important lessons about the union and government and organized crime.

I have two principle observations. I don't believe there is a place for government in unions. A union is for the members and it must be controlled by the members and not by any outside authority. Even less than the government, there is no place for organized crime in any union, for that matter, anywhere in society. I was a member and a shop steward during some of the darkest days of Local 560. I saw and experienced firsthand what organized crime could do to the local members. Members were intimidated from expressing their own opinions and disagreements. They were intimidated from participating in the union. I myself was intimidated and threatened. Sometimes it was subtle, and sometimes it was not so subtle.

The union was a burden that members suffered. It did not negotiate good contracts, good wages, or good benefits. It existed for the benefit of organized crime, members who controlled the union, but not the members. When the trusteeship was imposed in 1986, I had my doubts that it could work, but I was hopeful that it could. In my opinion it worked because we ultimately got the right person as trustee who had the right ideas of the purpose of the trusteeship, and he held to that idea no matter how difficult it was.

Choosing the Right Trustee

The right person was Mr. Ed Stier. Although Mr. Ed Stier was from a law enforcement background, he was cautious about imposing his own ideas on the union and the members. He was willing to listen and learn. And as you know, he hired experienced teamster, Frank Jackiewicz, a man who knew how to run a teamster's local.

The right idea, which Mr. Stier came to hold, was that the only purpose for the government and Local 560 was to eliminate organized crime and its influence to enable the members to resume the real control of the union in its own affairs. It seemed simple to state at the time. It seems simple to state this idea now, but it was not obvious at the beginning and it was often difficult to keep the government's role in the union so limited.

The temptation was always there for Mr. Stier to make decisions himself rather than allow the members to make those decisions. To his everlasting credit, Mr. Stier limited himself as much as possible to ridding the union of organized crime, and he allowed the members to regain control of the union. The key event in the trusteeship was Mr. Stier's decision to allow the members to elect an executive board to run the union.

Reforming Local 560

It was a difficult decision for me to run in that election. Over time, the executive board acted to remove officers who demonstrated they were still controlled by organized crime and officers who demonstrated that they would not or could not serve the interests of their members. We, the members, began to gradually resume control of the union. Members were able to express their opinions without fear or intimidation. With the participation of members, we began to negotiate good contracts, good wages, and good benefits. As we all did, we came to realize what a union should be. We came to understand what organized crime had taken away from us.

I am pleased to say that we at Local 560 now have the best wages that we do, the best benefits that we do and the best contracts in the area, bar none. We have doubled the retirement benefit. We have done that in just four years time. Our members now have increased health and welfare benefits, and we have some of the best in the country.

We now have come to the point not only that organized crime has been eliminated, but the members recognize what organized crime took from us. They never want that influence back into our union.

This fact is demonstrated by the recent election in Local 560. Almost 50 percent of the members voted in that election. The high turnout shows that the members are interested in the local union.

The slate that I ran on, the Brown slate, won 55 percent of the vote. We did this despite a constant barrage of campaign literature from our components that labeled us government men. Men who owe their loyalty to the government not to the members, but the members knew better. The slate headed by members associated with the old ways of Local 560 pulled only 25 percent of the vote. Clearly, the members have rejected organized crime and its influence but the transformation of the union came not without great cost. The trusteeship cost Local 560 more than $3 million. . . .

. . . The $3 million spent on the trusteeship meant that the union was not able to spend the money on things like organizing, education, member seminars, grievance procedures, and other membership benefits. This was a tremendous burden on this local, even though I believe the results ultimately justify their cost.

Mr. Chairman, and members of the committee, I come back to the lessons that we have learned. The only role for government can be to eliminate organized crime.

Two, the role of government must be limited to this goal. Government cannot become involved in the internal politics of the union. It must not act to favor one faction or another within that union.

Three, government supervision is fundamentally inconsistent with a union. The supervision is extremely costly both in terms of money and in terms of denying membership democratic control of the union through officers of their choosing, and that is very important. We must have that right to choose our own people. As soon as the influence of organized crime has ended, the government must go.

Thank you again for allowing me to testify. . . .

CHAPTER 2

Organized Crime and the International Drug Trade

Case Overview

United States v. Badalamenti (1986)

Popularly known as the "Pizza Connection," *United States v. Badalamenti* proved to be one of the longest and most complex organized crime trials of the 1980s. The trial for the twenty-two defendants lasted from October 1985 to February 1987 and included the testimony of over two hundred and seventy-five witnesses; the transcript for the trial ran forty thousand pages. Like the French Connection before it, the Pizza Connection consisted of an extensive network of organized crime figures from Sicily, Brazil, and the United States, involved in a conspiracy of narcotics distribution and money laundering. Once the shipments reached the Midwest United States, they were transported to the northeast. At the end of the pipeline were a number of pizza parlors, operating, in the public's mind, as legitimate businesses; in reality, however, they served as fronts for narcotics distribution.

Gaetano Badalamenti was at the center of the network, arranging shipments of heroin and cocaine to the American Midwest from a pay phone in Rio de Janeiro. Once the central figure in Sicilian organized crime, Badalamenti had been expelled from the Mafia Commission in 1978; but while other Mafia leaders had supposedly ordered his assassination, he continued to distribute drugs from Sicily until 1982. Eventually, Badalamenti relocated to Brazil where he established himself as a businessperson. He also continued to serve as the link between organized crime in Sicily and the United States. In essence, Badalamenti sat at the hub of a vast illegal business that arranged for the shipment of narcotics from sources in Sicily in exchange for cash payments from sources in the United States.

United States v. Badalamenti was significant for a number of reasons. Most importantly, the trial proved conclusively that organized crime was deeply involved in the distribution of heroin. A long-standing myth maintained that many within organized crime or the mafia refused involvement in the drug trade for ethical reasons. With *Badalamenti*, however, the connection between organized crime and the drug trade proved more extensive than anyone had imagined. An international organized crime network had built a pipeline that was capable of funneling as much as a ton and a half of heroin—worth $333 million dollars in street value—in a little over a year. Furthermore, by using pizza parlors as fronts for heroin distribution, American organized crime had built a domestic network right under the radar of law enforcement.

Badalamenti, however, also gave notice to how much law enforcement techniques had changed and revealed the significance of international cooperation. Much of the evidence used to convict the twenty-two defendants was gathered in thousands of wiretaps, transcribed into nine written volumes. During the trial, the prosecution relied on actors (the "pizza players") to read from these transcripts. FBI agents, who had followed and photographed the defendants over a number of years, supplied further evidence. Gathering evidence also required the cooperation of law enforcement from around the world, including agencies in Sicily, Brazil, Spain, and the United States.

Finally, *Badalamenti* proved noteworthy as yet another successful federal trial that significantly diminished the power of organized crime in the United States during the 1980s. While Badalamenti and other defendants appealed the convictions, a Federal Appeals Court upheld the majority of the sentences. Badalamenti was sentenced to life in prison and died of a heart attack on April 29, 2004.

> *"Because they were members of the Ma-*
> *fia and because they were trafficking in*
> *a contraband drug, they went to great*
> *lengths to conceal what it was that they*
> *were doing."*

Organized Crime Operates a Worldwide Drug Ring

United States Attorney Robert Stewart

Robert Stewart is the chief of the South Carolina Law Enforcement Division.

On the surface, the case of United States v. Badalamenti *(1986) seems extremely complex, consisting of twenty-two defendants, multiple witnesses, and thousands of wiretaps. According to Robert Stewart's opening statement, however, the case is quite simple, involving no more than the purchase and delivery of a specific product over a long period of time. Within these business arrangements, he says, individuals in the New York-New Jersey area contacted individuals around the world—in Sicily and South America—to purchase a product, which they in turn distributed for a substantial profit. Stewart contends that* United States v. Badalamenti *is unique, however, because the main product of exchange in these business arrangements is illegal drugs and because these illegal products are distributed by the Mafia. Because these activities are illegal, he contends, the Mafia developed an elaborate code and communicated by pay phones. By using the code and enforcing discipline within the*

Robert Stewart (U.S. Attorney), opening statement, *United States v. Badalamenti*, October 24, 1985. Quoted in James B. Jacobs, *Busting the Mob: United States v. Cosa Nostra.* New York: New York University, 1994, pp. 146–149. Copyright © 1994 by New York University Press. All rights reserved. Reproduced by permission.

organizations, the Mafia was able to conspire on multimillion dollar drug deals over a long period of time.

The indictment in this case charges 35 defendants, 22 of whom are here today, with conspiracy to violate the narcotics laws and related offenses involving the importation and distribution of narcotic drugs between the years 1975 and 1984. The case involves a number of individuals in addition to the 35 who are charged and the 22 who are actually here. You will hear a number of names during the course of this trial.

Certainly the case involves a number of events over a relatively long period of time. Yet the basic story of what occurred in this case is not very complicated. It is, stated in its simplest terms, the buying and selling of a commodity year in and year out, over and over again.

What I want to do in the next hour and perhaps 15 minutes is, first of all, to describe to you the basic nature of the business operation which is at the heart and the core of this case; secondly, to identify for you 11 individuals who are absolutely essential to this case and around whom all major events in this case occurred; thirdly, to go over the indictment with you in a bit more detail, identifying what all the charges are, identifying who all of the defendants are, some of the principal co-conspirators, and to describe for you what the role and what the function was of each of those defendants and co-conspirators in this particular narcotics operation; and finally, to review with you very briefly some of the evidence which you will be hearing during the coming weeks and months.

An International Business Operation

First, as to the basic elements of the business operation, the buying and selling of a commodity, a commodity which came from overseas. All that happened in this case was that a group of individuals in the New York-New Jersey metropolitan area formed a joint business venture. They got their friends and associates to come together as investors in the business venture and they called up some other friends and associates overseas and they said to those people overseas "Can you supply us with a commodity?" And the associate overseas called some of his friends and associates. Some they asked "Can you provide us with raw material?" Others, they said "Can you manufacture the raw material into the commodity?" And still others they asked to transport that commodity to America and to deliver it to the people who were the customers in America.

When the overseas supplier had done all those things, gotten the raw material, gotten it manufactured into the commodity and had it transported to the people in America, the people here sold the commodity at wholesale to their customers.

Now they had a big pile of money in front of them, 5s, 10s, 20s, 50s, $100 bills. No checks, no bank accounts. Just cash. And they did two things with that money. Part of it, a good part of it, they put into their pockets, because that was their profit, and it was a very, very handsome profit indeed. What remained they sent back to the overseas suppliers who had provided them with the commodity, because they had purchased that commodity almost always on credit or what in the trade is referred to as consignment.

When those dollars got back across the ocean into the hands of the overseas supplier he did four things with that money. Part of it he gave to the person or persons who provided the raw material, part of it he gave to the person or persons who manufactured that raw material into the final commodity, part of it he gave to the people who transported that commodity to the customers in America, and the rest of it he put in his pocket.

The Mafia-Narcotics Connection

That was all that happened in this case, month in, month out, year in and year out, throughout the nine years that are charged in the indictment.

What makes this particular business operation unusual and unique and, indeed, the subject of this prosecution is that the commodity in question was massive amounts of contraband narcotic drugs, heroin and cocaine, and secondly, that the individuals, every one of the people who was involved in the process of buying and selling these commodities, were members or associates of the Mafia, the Mafia in Sicily or the Mafia in the United States.

Because they were members of the Mafia and because they were trafficking in a contraband drug, they went to great lengths to conceal what it was that they were doing, and so you will not see one of these defendants pick up the telephone in his office—and all of the defendants had legitimate businesses and they all had telephones in their legitimate businesses—you will not see them pick up those telephones and call an overseas supplier and say, "Send me 22 kilograms of cocaine next week."

What you are going to see instead are people standing on street corners in the dead of winter, shivering and shaking for an hour waiting for a pay telephone call to come from somebody in Sicily or somebody in Illinois or somebody in Brazil who is also going to be using a pay telephone.

And when the call finally comes you're not going to hear ordinary intelligible sentences of a person ordering a commodity on terms and price and conditions. What you will hear is people talking in codes about shirts and shoes and pants and the old pants and the new pants and the architect and the engineer and the work over there and plants and potatoes and cheese, anything but what they are really talking about, which is heroin and cocaine and kilograms and dollars and cents.

You will be in a unique position because you will hear these conversations over pay telephones and you will know what the codes are. As a matter of fact, by the end of this case you will know the codes better than many of the defendants, because they had great difficulties during the course of the conspiracy keeping the codes straight, and consequently not infrequently you will see a person standing out on a street corner and never getting the call because somebody has made a mistake in the code and the call is going to another telephone somewhere halfway around the world. But you will have the benefit of knowing what the codes are and of understanding exactly and precisely what it is that these people are doing in their telephone conversations and in their other movements.

Smuggling and the Mafia

The evidence will demonstrate that there are two basic themes to this case. One of those themes involves the dynamics of smuggling, the smuggling of massive quantities of heroin and cocaine into the United States on a protracted and systematic basis and the smuggling of massive amounts of United States currency out of the United States to the overseas suppliers. Indeed, during just part of 1982 and 1983 just one of the overseas operations located in Sicily earmarked over a ton and a half of pure heroin for consignment to the core group individuals who were importing the drugs and distributing the drugs here in the New York metropolitan area. That ton and a half of heroin, pure heroin, had a wholesale value of over $333 million, a third of a billion dollars, in the space of a little over a year.

Between the years 1980 and 1983, the evidence will demonstrate that over $40 million was smuggled out of the United States into Switzerland for distribution to some of the suppliers in Sicily, and that does not count money that was smuggled out of the United States to pay for other overseas suppliers in Brazil.

Smuggling, then, is one of the basic themes of this case. The second basic theme of this case involves the dynamics of the Mafia, a secret criminal organization both there and in the

United States which provided the cement that held together the components of this conspiracy year in and year out throughout the nine years charged in this indictment.

It was the Mafia organization's discipline and protocol and rules of order which enabled the co-conspirators in this case to deal with one another a third of the way around the world from each other, to enter into agreements which although having no ability to enforce their contracts in the law were nevertheless binding upon the members and associates of the secret society, agreements involving millions of dollars in cash and millions of dollars in product.

It was the Mafia discipline which enabled members to take a package containing a million dollars in cash or a million dollars in heroin and go in the dead of night and walk down a dark alley to meet with somebody confident that they would not be ambushed and robbed by the person that they were going to meet because there was a code of honor among these people that bound them to honor their obligations.

That was the discipline and the organization that made this conspiracy possible, that brought these people together and that held them together year in and year out and gave them a very, very distinct advantage over any other competitor that lacked that basic organization.

> *"Although we hold here that the length and complexity of this trial did not deprive appellants of their right to due process, we do have misgivings about trials of this magnitude."*

The Federal Court's Decision: The Defendants in *Badalamenti* Received a Fair Trial

Lawrence W. Pierce

Lawrence W. Pierce was originally appointed by President Richard Nixon in 1971, and served twenty-four years as a federal judge.

Following the conviction of the majority of the defendants in United States v. Badalamenti *(1986), a number of defendants, including Badalamenti, appealed the decision in* United States v. Filippo Casamento. *The defendants' appeal argued that because of the length and complexity of the case, and because of the violence that surrounded the case, they had not received a fair trial. While Judge Pierce's decision agrees that the case was both complex and lengthy, he argues that the jury had proven itself competent in following the details of the case. He says that the very fact that the jury requested transcripts from the trial supports the idea that they had made a conscientious effort to comprehend fully the material before making a decision. Furthermore, Pierce argues that the air of violence surrounding the trial did*

Lawrence W. Pierce, decision, *United States v. Filippo Casamento*, United States Court of Appeal, Second Circuit, January 26, 1989. http://cases.justia.com.

not prejudice the jury against the defendants. On several occasions, in fact, the court questioned jury members regarding outside influences; in each case, the court determined that the jury had not been prejudiced by news sources. While Pierce upholds the original decision in Badalamenti, *he nonetheless expresses the need to limit the length and complexity of future trials whenever possible.*

The government contends that the alleged criminal events herein began in Sicily in the 1970s when members of the Sicilian Mafia decided to begin shipping narcotics to the United States. These shipments came from two places, Sicily and South America. In Sicily, Mafia members imported morphine base from Turkey, refined it, and smuggled the heroin they produced into the New York metropolitan area. Among the Sicilian Mafia members who the government contends were responsible for shipping the heroin and developing a distribution network in the United States were defendant Giuseppe Soresi and appellants Lorenzo Devardo and Giovanni Cangialosi. According to the government, the source of narcotics from South America was appellant Gaetano Badalamenti, a fugitive living in Brazil who was allegedly the deposed head of the Sicilian Mafia and who, in connection with this prosecution, later was extradited from Spain.

It is contended that Badalamenti sent narcotics to the Midwest, where the drugs allegedly were distributed by defendants Pietro Alfano and Salvatore Evola and appellants Emanuele Palazzolo, Giuseppe Vitale and Giuseppe Trupiano. The midwestern distributors delivered narcotics to a distribution group in the New York area. This New York group, comprised of members of the American Mafia, or La Cosa Nostra, also received heroin shipments from Sicily.

Further, according to the government, appellant Salvatore Catalano led the New York group, closely assisted by defendant Giuseppe Ganci and appellants Giuseppe Lamberti, Salvatore Lamberti, Salvatore Greco and Salvatore Mazzurco. Allegedly, Catalano also worked closely with defendant Gaetano Mazzara and appellant Frank Castronovo, who the government claims were two Sicilian Mafia members stationed in New Jersey.

The government asserts that the New York group sold narcotics to secondary wholesalers, such as appellant Filippo Casamento and defendant Benito Zito, and that to finance its importation of narcotics, the New York group relied on payments from investors, such as appellants Francesco Polizzi and Giovanni Ligammari.

In addition, according to the government, as part of the conspiracy's money laundering operation, appellants Catalano, Castronovo, Ganci, Salvatore Salamone and his brother, defendant Filippo Salamone, accumulated the conspiracy's cash proceeds in pizza parlors, and then either smuggled the cash out of the country in suitcases or laundered it through a maze of bank accounts. The government asserts that the money was deposited in Swiss bank accounts, and from there went to conspirators in Italy or to a man known as Musullulu, who the government claims supplied the conspirators with morphine base from Turkey.

Having briefly described the alleged criminal activities, we now turn to a discussion of the various issues raised on appeal.

Questions Pertaining to Due Process

A principal issue raised on appeal is whether the joint trial of the numerous defendants deprived the individual defendants of their right to due process. To support their claims of lack of due process, appellants mainly point to (1) the length and complexity of the trial, (2) the spillover prejudice which allegedly resulted from the joinder of the defendants, and (3) the publicity and the alleged atmosphere of violence which surrounded the trial.

By any standard, the magnitude of this trial was extraordinary. Based on a multi-count indictment which charged thirty-five defendants, the joint trial of twenty-one defendants spanned more than seventeen months, produced more than forty thousand pages of trial transcript, and, according to defense counsel, involved the introduction of thousands of exhibits and the testimony of more than two hundred and seventy-five witnesses.

During the course of the trial, Judge Leval allowed the government to display charts to the jury which, through graphs, maps or brief written descriptions, summarized the evidence the government had presented. Much of this evidence was uncontested, consisting of the testimony of government agents regarding observations made during surveillance, transcripts of intercepted telephone conversations, and seized items such as guns or money. Before a chart was shown to the jury, the judge gave the defendants a chance to object to its contents. In some instances, he directed that changes be made in the contents of a chart in response to a defendant's objection. Several times during the trial, the district judge instructed the jury that the charts were not evidence. He also told the jurors that they were free to disregard the contents of the charts if they chose to do so. The judge repeated these instructions during his charge.

Near the end of the trial, the government compiled a binder which contained reproductions of the summary charts which had been displayed to the jury during the trial. During its deliberations, the jury requested and received copies of this binder, as well as the entire trial transcript, specifically identified items of evidence, and also a blackboard, chalk and an eraser.

Appellants argue that the length and complexity of the trial prevented the jury from adequately remembering and evaluating the evidence. They argue that because the jury could not remember the evidence sufficiently, it had to rely uncritically on the government's summary charts. Appellants contend that, because the jury was unable to evaluate the evidence independently, severance was required, and that the district court's refusal to sever the trial, as requested, deprived them of due process. . . .

Questions Pertaining to Length and Complexity

We do not agree that the length and complexity of this trial caused the appellants substantial prejudice. First of all, we have no reason to believe that the jury lacked the intellectual capacity to meet the task before it. Although the jury had to evaluate a tremendous amount of evidence, the nature of the evidence and the legal concepts involved in the case were not extraordinarily difficult to comprehend, as they might be, for example, in a complex anti-trust case involving abstruse economic theories or an employment discrimination case involving technical statistical evidence and formulae. Here, the jury was required to grasp the legal significance of shipments of narcotics, sales of narcotics, and transfers of money.

The clearest indication that the jury was able to evaluate the evidence, despite its being voluminous, is provided by the jury's verdicts themselves. We have held that in a multi-defendant case, a mix of guilty and not guilty verdicts is some indication that the jury was able to sift through voluminous evidence and differentiate among various defendants. Here, the jury's not guilty verdicts on certain counts inform us that the jury differentiated among the defendants. The clear distinctions the jury drew among the defendants strongly suggest that it was indeed able to evaluate the evidence critically and follow the instructions of the trial judge.

Another indication that the jury was able to evaluate the evidence fairly was the apparent effort it made during its deliberations to parse and weigh the evidence. The jury's requests for the entire trial transcript, for various items in evidence, and for a blackboard, chalk, and eraser, as well as copies of the summary chart book, suggest that the jurors, rather than despairing in the face of the daunting amount of evidence, accepted their arduous role and diligently and conscientiously proceeded over the six-day period of deliberations to meet their responsibilities as fact-finders. We believe that a jury overwhelmed by the evidence would not have manifested the interest shown here in making such an effort. . . .

In addition to their argument that the jury could not fairly evaluate the great volume of evidence, appellants argue that the length and complexity of the trial placed a great burden on the jurors, and they suggest that this burden may have caused the jurors to harbor resentment toward the defendants. Although the trial was undoubtedly burdensome for the jury, and one juror, later excused, did express resentment towards the defendants, we do not believe that the burden caused appellants to suffer substantial prejudice. We base this conclusion in large part (1) on the verdicts the jury rendered, and (2) on the apparently careful way in which the jury evaluated the evidence, both of which support Judge Leval's characterization of the jury's performance during the trial as "fair, open-minded, [and] conscientious."

Outlining Limits for Mega-Trials

Although we hold here that the length and complexity of this trial did not deprive appellants of their right to due process, we do have misgivings about trials of this magnitude. We are aware that lengthy multi-defendant trials may provide certain benefits in terms of the judicial system. We recognize the evident disadvantages which can occur in these mega-trials; we also recognize that district judges must retain a considerable degree of discretion in determining whether, on balance, the fair administration of justice will be better served by one aggregate trial of all indicted defendants or by two or more trials of groups of defendants. However, we believe that some benchmarks ought to be set out to guide the exercise of that discretion. First, the district judge should elicit from the prosecutor a good-faith estimate of the time reasonably anticipated to present the government's case. Though the prosecutor's estimate should not become the subject of a contested hearing, the judge need not accept the estimate without question but should be free to make an independent assessment based on various factors including the number of defendants, the time and territorial scope of the crimes charged, the number of witnesses likely to be called, and the number and size of exhibits likely to be introduced, including wiretaps.

In those cases where the judge determines that the time for presentation of the prosecution's case will exceed four months, the judge should oblige the prosecutor to present a reasoned basis to support a conclusion that a joint trial of all the defendants is more consistent with the fair administration of justice than some manageable division of the case into separate trials for groups of defendants. In determining whether the prosecutor has made an adequate showing, the judge should weigh the interests of the prosecution, the defendants, the jurors, the court, and the public. Again, we do not contemplate a contested hearing nor precise findings on this subject. A submission by the prosecutor, a response by the defendants seeking a severance, and a conclusion by the judge will suffice. . . .

Finally, in assessing the appropriate number of defendants for any trial in which the prosecution's case is likely to require more than four months to present, the judge should oblige the prosecutor to make an especially compelling justification for a joint trial of more than ten defendants. Even in the event that the aggregate time for separate trials would not be less than the time for a joint trial of all defendants, there are significant advantages to be achieved. The lives of each group of jurors would be imposed upon for a shorter time, there would be a smaller group of defense counsel in each trial with a consequent reduction in trial disputes, the trial judge would have a more manageable task, and the jurors' ability to focus on individual defendants would be enhanced. While the prosecution's estimate that separate trials will each require all of the evidence presented at a joint trial is often not borne out when severances occur, we note that in this case there is a striking example of an instance when a contrary estimate was made. One of the original co-defendants herein was Giuseppi Baldinucci. Instead of enduring a seventeen-month trial, he was severed at the instance of the government and brought to trial on narrower charges. He was convicted after a trial lasting just seven days. . . .

An Alleged Atmosphere of Violence

Further, appellants argue that the publicity and the alleged atmosphere of violence which surrounded the joint trial rendered it unfair. To support this argument appellants point to the following: (1) the government's allegation, in its opening statement to the jury, that Catalano was involved in the 1979 murder of the alleged Mafia figure Carmine Galante; (2) the great deal of publicity which surrounded the trial in general; (3) the publicity surrounding the murder, approximately two and one-half months into the trial, of the alleged Mafia figure Paul Castellano; (4) the violent death, about fourteen months into the trial, of defendant Gaetano Mazzara and the publicity which surrounded this event; (5) the non-fatal shooting of defendant Pietro Alfano, which occurred during the summation stage of the trial, and the publicity which surrounded this event; and (6) the government's display to the jury of various guns seized from Greco's pizzeria. As we discuss below, after reviewing the record, we conclude that the publicity and the alleged atmosphere of violence which surrounded this case did not deprive appellants of due process.

The district court stated that it was prejudicial for the government to mention in its opening argument Catalano's alleged connection to the Galante murder. Rather than grant a mistrial however, Judge Leval instructed the jury that the Galante murder was not a part of the trial and that the jury should not consider it. Although the defendants, as the district court acknowledged, were prejudiced by the government's mention of the Galante murder, we do not believe that this prejudice was substantial enough to have deprived appellants of their right to due process. First, given the care with which the jury apparently considered the evidence, we think the government's prejudicial statement did not have a significant impact. Second, the district judge gave the jury a proper instruction. Third, without more, we presume, as we must, that the jury followed the judge's instruction not to consider the government's mention of the Galante murder. In short, in light of the jury's apparent care in weighing the evidence, coupled with the judge's instruction to the jury, we hold that the government's statement in its opening argument did not deprive defendants of a fair trial.

Without a doubt, this trial attracted a great deal of media attention. We do not believe, however, that this publicity rendered the trial unfair. On several occasions, Judge Leval instructed the jury not to pay attention to anything which appeared in the media concerning the trial. In the absence of evidence to the contrary, we will presume the jury followed these admonitions and avoided exposure to news reports about the trial. Some warrant for this presumption is provided by the fact that several times during the trial the judge conducted voir dire [French, to question a juror] of the jury to satisfy himself that the jurors had followed his instructions and had indeed avoided news reports about the case, e.g., on January 13, 1986, following the reported appearance in the *New York Times* of an "article" by former President Ronald Reagan which concerned organized crime and which favorably mentioned then United States Attorney Rudolph Giuliani; on January 16, 1986, following the reported appearance of a cover story in

New York magazine about Nicholas Pileggi's book *Wise Guy: Life in the Mob*; on February 5, 1986, following the reported appearance in the *New York Post* of an article recounting testimony from the trial; and on December 3, 1986, following the Mazzara murder. A district judge has substantial discretion in determining whether potentially prejudicial publicity has affected a jury's impartiality, and a conclusion that the jury remained impartial will not be overturned on appeal absent an abuse of discretion. Here, in light of the district judge's instructions and inquiries of the jury via voir dire, and his considered conclusions as to the jurors' impartiality, we believe that he acted well within his discretion in deciding that the publicity which the trial generated did not affect the jurors' ability to serve fairly.

"All the big Sicilian Mafia players on the New York scene were helping to smuggle the aliens in."

The Long Reach of the International Sicilian Mafia

Claire Sterling

Claire Sterling was a journalist and author whose works included The Terror Network *and* Octopus: The Long Reach of the International Sicilian Mafia.

The international dimension of United States v. Badalamenti *(1986) required the cooperation of law enforcement from Europe, South America, and the United States. As Claire Sterling explains, the heroin pipeline that became known as the "Pizza Connection" reached from Sicily to multiple American pizza parlors. In the United States, organized crime families utilized illegal Sicilian immigrants to work in pizza parlors as both everyday laborers and as drug dealers. Organized crime families also made money by investing in the supply business, providing chains with the multiple items (cheese, meat, and sauce) needed to make pizzas.*

Operating in Brazil, ex-Sicilian Mafia figure Gaetano Badalamenti formed a central link in the chain, arranging drug deals by payphone with trusted relatives located in the Midwest. For a long time, however, law enforcement was unable to identify Badalamenti. Once DEA (Drug Enforcement Administration) agents made this connection, however, the United States and

*Italian police were able to apprehend Badalamenti in Spain. Al-
though he was wanted in both countries, it was agreed that the
United States would extradite Badalamenti while Italy would
extradite Tommaso Buscetta, another central figure in the Sicilian Mafia.*

The Sicilian Mafia did not invent the pizza, but made richly
inventive use of it. Sooner or later, from 1963 onward,
nearly all Cosa Nostra troops in America got into the pizza
business, sheltered behind it, washed their drug money
through it, skimmed the cash take, worked it to extort payoffs
by arson, acid, bombing, and murder, pulled a thousand scams
on its customers, and passed dope on from one of its kitchen
doors to another. Two decades passed before the FBI discovered that Sicilian Mafiosi were running "a sizeable portion of
the heroin importation business to the United States" through
these pizza parlors. The violence and extortion had attracted
some attention, but the names and faces had not.

Mafiosi usually muscled their way into the business. The
Cherry Hill Gambinos picked up the pizza franchise at the
Cherry Hill Mall in southern New Jersey by burning the place
down, firebombing the manager's car, and then giving him a
call. "What I did to your car, I'm going to do to you if you
don't do what you're told," said the voice on the phone. "I'm
gonna take a gun in my hand and blow your face off. Get
wise. Get smart. Close up. Turn your keys in."

Not that they were necessarily averse to peaceful surrender.
The Sicilian Mafia's branch manager in Washington, D.C., a
convivial host named Luciano Fiumefreddo, claimed to have
acquired his nicest pizza parlor in Prince George County,
Maryland, merely by asking. "I couldn't sleep one night, so I
drove over there and saw the Landover Mall. I was so over-
come by its beauty that I waited in the parking lot all night,
and then went in to ask if I could rent the place," he explained.

Fiumefreddo, who owned six more pizza parlors around the nation's capital, had bought a dozen others up and down the eastern seaboard since arriving from Sicily in October 1963. . . . Fellow fugitives were doing the same from coast to coast. They worked hard, sifting flour and kneading dough, hauling cartons and swabbing floors, opening early and closing late. To outsiders, they were indistinguishable from thousands of honest Sicilian immigrants in the trade.

Hiding in Public View

There was nothing like hiding in full public view. All America could watch them at work without a twinge of suspicion. The public loved these new Sicilian-run eateries, springing up like mushrooms after rain. They were fast—that was probably the secret of the traffickers' unique success in devising just this system for just this country of fast-food fans—as well as cheap and less poisonous than many. The pizzeria run in Oregon, Illinois, by a Pizza Connection defendant was missed after his arrest. "He used to put real bacon in his pizzas—not bacon bits," a customer recalled.

The police rarely bothered these establishments, and then only because of so many illegal Sicilian aliens in their employ. Nine out of every ten reported by the U.S. Immigration and Naturalization Service were found working in pizzerias. The phenomenon puzzled law enforcement agencies. As time went by, they began to think that drugs might have something to do with it, but that was as far as they got.

All the big Sicilian Mafia players on the New York scene were helping to smuggle the aliens in: the Cherry Hill Gambinos, Emmanuele Adamita (their main heroin courier), Salvatore Inzerillo (Palermo's future heroin king), Enzo and Antonino Napoli, [Tommaso] Buscetta, and the whole crowd of their close associates. For agents accustomed to minding their own backyard, however, these were just the "geeps," or "zips," the "f---ing siggies" who didn't count. It was taken for granted that some American Mafia Family must be running the aliens in; probably the Gambino Family, since Carlo Gambino's brother Paolo was clearly in charge.

"I came to New York in 1970, and was put on a special squad to cover the Carlo Gambino Family," said James Kallstrom, the FBI's crack Mafia watcher in New York.

We had a case on his brother Paolo then. Paolo was very rich, but not from their normal activities. He was bringing in the aliens.

We saw the whole network; they were setting up the heroin net all through the sixties and seventies, right under our noses. They were all in cheese—making mozzarella and selling to pizzerias that were popping up everywhere. . . . I followed their cheese trucks to pizza parlors in New York, New Jersey, Connecticut. They had hundreds of pizzerias, all run by illegal aliens just in from Palermo. . . . We thought the Gambino Family must be bringing in hundreds of Sicilian illegals, paying them a little and forming an army—but what for?

We thought it could be drugs; enough dope was seized in casual arrests to suggest a drug ring. But the association wasn't clear.

Sicilian Illegals

The New Jersey State Police had assembled many more facts by 1973, but hardly gotten closer to the truth. The exceptional influx of Sicilian illegals was "harder to comprehend from one day to the next," the police intelligence analyst observed. Several thousand aliens were now known to have come through. Though many were under indictment for murder and mayhem at home, they were "unidentifiable in the U.S.": nonpersons with no fingerprints or Social Security numbers on file. Obviously, they could serve some criminal purpose. But which?

Sicilians appeared to have no trouble getting into the country. A good number used throwaway forged passports and lied their way in on their own. Thousands more were ferried in smoothly by an organized international ring. As the New Jersey police described it, a certain travel agent in Sicily would collect $500 a head, sell the customers an airline ticket to Montreal, and give them a business card for the Laurentian Hotel there or the Royal Motel in Lachine, Quebec. Upon checking in, they would be told to wait for "Salvatore" (or "Paolo" or "Giuseppe"), who would collect another $500 and take them over the border.

The Canadian-U.S. border below Montreal runs for 1,200 miles from the Atlantic Ocean to the Great Lakes, with dozens of small waterways and backwoods roads in between. Only a hundred border guards were stationed on the U.S. side in those years, from Maine to Erie, Pennsylvania; and fewer than twenty were on duty at any given time. Eluding them was child's play.

Once across, the illegals would scatter according to their means. Those with the right connections took over pizzerias, usually with start-up money from fellow Mafiosi already settled in. The others worked in the pizza shops as slave labor. They would be paid a few dollars a week and be bedded down in a dormitory or on the shop floor. Without papers, or knowing a word of English, they were prisoners.

Eventually, deserving illegals would get a *sistemazione*, as Italians call it; the Mafia would arrange to make them legal. The methods varied from simple forgery or fraud to methodical bribery on Capitol Hill. One way was a quickie marriage to an American girl; the groom would get naturalized citizenship in six months followed by divorce, the bride $1,500. Another was the falsification of petitions for residence permits. Cheese makers were given a much higher priority on the waiting list than manual laborers, for instance. Thus, by faking his employment references—among other things—a prime Sicilian trafficker and pizza franchiser, Michael Piancone, became a lawful resident of the United States. . . .

Organized Crime

The Pizza Business

The pizza circuit used its own suppliers, with a monopoly on all the necessities for the pizza industry—ovens, oils, tomato sauce, meat, mushrooms, mozzarella cheese. ("How come you don't make mozzarella?" the FBI's James Kallstrom once asked a Kraft Cheese Company officer, who winked in reply.) Supplies were "totally controlled, from the time they are contracted for in a foreign country to the time they are delivered to the ultimate consumer in the United States," stated a U.S. Customs report on the West Coast.

Many American Mafiosi had been taken into partnership, joining forces with their Sicilian counterparts, much as two corporate giants might do. Joe Bonanno, a pioneer in the field, was locked into the circuit with his Grande Cheese Company in Wisconsin (a manufacturer of national importance) and an intricate web of subsidiaries. His sometime partners, the Falcone brothers of Sicily and Brooklyn, ran an elaborate network of dairies as well as an interstate King of Pizza chain.

Carlo Gambino's brother Paolo and nephew by marriage Frank Ferro owned another cheese-making network, Ferro Cheese, covering a territory from Virginia to Maine. Carlo Gambino's brother-in-law and future successor, Paul Castellano, was a major meat supplier.

All crossed paths with a singular outfit called Roma Foods, which did business in cash with 650 pizzerias from South Plainfield, New Jersey, to Jacksonville, Florida, and Dallas, Texas. Its Sicilian-born owner was Louis Piancone, one of two brothers of unusual interest in this story.

The Piancones came from Carato Bari, Sicily. Louis had married (and later divorced) an American tourist overseas; his brother Michael, the illegal with fake cheese maker's credentials, had slipped into the United States in 1963. Early partners in the pizza business, they had branched out in different directions by the end of that decade.

Michael Piancone owned a four-state chain of Piancone Pizza Palaces, sold franchises for others, and hired more illegal Sicilian aliens than anybody in the state of New Jersey. Several of his pizza parlors were notorious heroin bases. The biggest heroin seizure on record up to 1971 was made that year in one of his New Jersey Pizza Palaces: eighty-six kilos, shipped from Palermo by Gaetano Badalamenti. . . .

Worldwide Connections

The money discovered in the Pizza Connection case was irrefutable proof that the Sicilian Mafia was operating on a worldwide scale, and could only be dealt with across national boundaries. The FBI could not have followed the trail without substantial help from Italy, Switzerland, Spain, France, Canada, West Germany, and Luxembourg. Italy and Switzerland especially were so closely involved that major Pizza Connection trials were held in both countries for money washers caught on their soil.

And the money made the case against the twenty-two defendants in New York. The millions of dollars changing hands and leaving the country—in cash, in small bills—was crushing evidence to put before a jury. The remaining burden of proof depended largely on saturation surveillance, at which the FBI excelled. A thousand roles of film, fifty-five thousand wiretaps, a million man-hours of surveillance, tipped the balance.

For all the bureau's manpower and resources, however, its agents could not have decoded what they saw and heard in America without knowing what was going on in Sicily.

Sicily was in the midst of a Mafia war, a source of monumental confusion to American agents who had enough trouble as it was. The Corleonesi [a faction of the Sicilian Mafia] and their allies had taken over the Cupola [a Mafia governing body] and its heroin pipeline in Palermo [a city in Southern Italy], impelling the Sicilian Mafiosi in New York to proceed with almost hysterical caution.

The Reemergence of Badalamenti

The big losers in Palermo were nearly all dead by the end of 1981, leaving survivors like Gaetano Badalamenti in an awkward position. Expelled from the Cupola in 1978, presumably sentenced to be shot on sight, he had nevertheless continued to run drugs out of Sicily until 1982. Then he was apparently obliged to take off and conduct his business elsewhere, confounding everyone on the Pizza case.

[Tommaso] Buscetta, [a Sicilian Mafioso], testifying at the Pizza trial, swore that Badalamenti was running for his life. If so, he stopped along the way to make a lot of phone calls. Nobody knew where he was calling from; mostly from a public phone booth in Rio de Janeiro, it turned out. The FBI's wizards finally traced the calls to and from tiny towns like Temperance, Michigan (south of Detroit), right off the map in the American Middle West. Apparently, he would trust only his own intermediaries there for his substantial deals with the Sicilians in Brooklyn. To all appearances, the Sicilians shunned Badalamenti even as they bought quantities of heroin and cocaine from him. Supposedly they would have to kill him if they caught him; plainly, they didn't want to catch him.

But if it was true that Badalamenti was running for his life, he could have had no dealings with the Sicilian Mafia's new rulers in Palermo. In reality, he must have been dealing with them, or for them. In fact, he practically gave the secret away, in the single most meaningful conversation among the thousands overheard by the FBI.

Badalamenti was talking to a nephew in Oregon, Illinois, from his favorite phone booth in Brazil, in February 1984. The question was whether to use some foreign supplier who clearly was *not* working with, or for, the Sicilian Mafia, someone who "did not have the license" to bring narcotics into the United States. "It is he who needs us," Badalamenti explained to his nephew. "He does not have an importer's license. *We have the license.*" There, in four words, was the definition of the Sicilian Mafia's heroin franchise. The "we" could only mean that the outcast Badalamenti still enjoyed his trading privileges, if only at a discreet distance.

Badalamenti as the "Mystery Man"

The Pizza trial was over, and a great deal more was known, before the full import of Badalamenti's phrase sank in. Louis Freeh [assistant U.S. attorney on the case], going back over this ground with me in 1987, drew the logical conclusion: Badalamenti was referring to the historic decision made by the American and Sicilian Mafias in 1957 at the Hotel des Palmes in Palermo.

This was far beyond anybody's thinking when FBI agents were listening in on Badalamenti's phone calls in 1984. They had heard all about him from the Italians by then, but he was still a hopeless mystery, known merely as "the Uncle" in hundreds of baffling wiretaps. Nobody knew where he was, or whose uncle he was, or *who* he was, until the DEA's [Drug Enforcement Administration] Mona Ewell finally matched his disembodied voice on the phone to an answering nephew's in Temperance, Michigan.

Badalamenti was not the only supplier for Catalano's crowd; at least two Mafia Families were shipping directly from Sicily. But he was a storybook Man of Honor, the former crowned head of the Sicilian Mafia, a notorious drug trafficker all his grown life; and in 1984, he was hot.

The phone traffic was frenetic in the early months of that year, from Rio to Oregon, Illinois, to New York and back. Badalamenti was preparing to send twenty kilos of cocaine to the Brooklyn ring via his Midwest nephews: the first clear chance in four years to catch them all in the act. But then, the chance came to catch Badalamenti himself, and the Americans went for it. They had the money, the heroin sold to a DEA agent in Philadelphia, the damning reunion in a Bagheria farmhouse, the thousand rolls of film and fifty-five thousand wiretaps—

the twenty-two defendants of their choice wrapped up. Badalamenti would be their ultimate reward for all the years of torment.

When the Americans caught up with him in Madrid [Spain], in April 1984, the Italian police were there as well. Both countries had come to the end of exhaustive investigations under way since 1980. Both were preparing to put the Sicilian Mafia on trial for a continuing criminal conspiracy dating back to 1975. Both wanted Badalamenti, but they were close enough then to make a swap.

Tommaso Buscetta, arrested in Brazil the previous autumn, was awaiting extradition to either the United States or Italy. Second only to Badalamenti as one of the world's most wanted drug traffickers, he was another prize catch. Both countries wanted him too. By mutual consent, the Americans took Badalamenti and the Italians got Buscetta.

| "More than any other case, Badalamenti demonstrates how formidable an opponent to organized crime law enforcement has become."

Badalamenti Confirmed the Mafia's Involvement with Drug Trafficking

James B. Jacobs

James B. Jacobs is a legal scholar and law professor at New York University of Law.

United States v. Badalamenti *(1986) was popularly known as the "Pizza Connection," and revealed an extensive connection between organized crime around the world and drug trafficking. Following a lengthy investigation, a number of indictments were handed down, including one against Gaetano Badalamenti, a former member of the Sicilian Mafia. James B. Jacobs points out in this excerpt that the trial was unique for both its number of defendants (twenty-two) and length (seventeen months). Following the trial, the jury convicted the majority of the defendants on most of the charges, and Judge Pierre Leval set a lengthy sentence and fine for Badalamenti. While the defendants presented an appeal that questioned the atmosphere of the trial, the sufficiency of the evidence, and restitution penalties, the Appeals Court made only minor changes to the sentences. Besides exposing organized crime's extensive involvement with the interna-*

James B. Jacobs, Christopher Panarella and Jay Worthington, *Busting the Mob: United States v. Cosa Nostra.* New York: New York University Press, 1994, pp. 129–144.

tional drug trade, Jacobs contends that Badalamenti *revealed law enforcement's ability to contest organized crime with modern technology like wiretapping.*

*U*nited States v. *Badalamenti* exposed a heroin-trafficking conspiracy that emerged in the aftermath of the breakup of the French Connection in the early 1970s. The case came to be known as the "Pizza Connection case" because several of the defendants used pizzerias as fronts for engaging in heroin distribution. It was the longest organized crime trial and culminated the largest and most complex of the decade's organized crime investigations. *Badalamenti* exposed organized crime's involvement in drug trafficking and the extensive cooperation between the American Cosa Nostra and the Sicilian Mafia. The case also demonstrated the extraordinary efforts American and foreign law enforcement agencies are capable of in their pursuit of organized crime.

The Indictment and Defendants

The final superseding indictment, filed on February 19, 1985, charged thirty-five defendants with conspiracy to import drugs and to evade banking and money-laundering statutes. The entire trafficking network allegedly involved over two hundred additional participants. In addition to the *Badalamenti* defendants, some conspirators were prosecuted in Italy and Switzerland; others were later prosecuted in *United States v. Adamita* [(1988)].

The indictment charged numerous specific violations of currency importation and transaction reporting statutes; thirty-one defendants were charged with participating in a RICO [Racketeer Influenced and Corrupt Organizations Act] conspiracy, and ten were charged with managing a "continuing criminal enterprise."

The indictment named as defendants senior Mafia figures, including Gaetano Badalamenti and Salvatore Catalano, along with lower-level participants in the drug traffic, such as investors, drug couriers, and messengers responsible for coordinating the conspiracy's far-flung factions. In effect, *United States v. Badalamenti* brought to trial an international Cosa Nostra drug-trafficking operation.

Twenty of the defendants were connected to two groups: eight relatives of Gaetano Badalamenti, once head of the Sicilian Mafia commission, and twelve members and associates of the Sicilian Mafia, some of whom had become important figures in New York's Bonanno crime family. Two defendants, couriers of money and messages, belonged to neither of these factions.

Gaetano Badalamenti was the most prominent defendant. As a result of the Sicilian Mafia wars of the early 1970s, the Corleonesi crime family had driven him out of Italy and murdered numerous members of his family. The indictment charged that he had conspired to export narcotics from Brazil, where he was living, to the United States. Seven of his relatives were also named as defendants: Salvatore Evola, a contractor in Temperance, Michigan, accused of being an investor and distributor in the operation; Emanuele Palazzolo and Pietro Alfano, pizzeria owners in Wisconsin and Michigan, accused of being investors and organizers of the trafficking; Giuseppe Trupiano, Giuseppe Vitale, and Vincenzo Randazzo, accused of participating as couriers; and Vito Badalamenti, Gaetano's son, accused of assisting his father in the conspiracy.

Salvatore Catalano, a capo in the Bonanno family, was the highest-ranking Cosa Nostra member of the trial's New York defendants. He was also allegedly a member of the Sicilian Mafia and was accused of running the Bonanno drug importation business, which purchased drugs from the Corleonesi organization in Sicily and from Badalamenti's organization in Brazil. The indictment charged Giuseppe Ganci with being a key organizer of the drug importation and distribution joint venture in America. Salvatore Lamberti, a member of the Sicilian Mafia's Borgetto family, his cousin Giuseppe Lamberti, a partner of Catalano and Ganci, and Giuseppe's brother-in-law Salvatore Mazzurco, another Catalano/Ganci partner, were named as investors in the drug business and charged with negotiating purchases of drugs in Sicily for the Catalano/Ganci group. The indictment charged Gaetano Mazzara and Frank Castronovo with storing drug money for the consortium in their New Jersey restaurant. Salvatore Greco, a New Jersey pizzeria owner and the brother of Sicilian Mafia boss Leonardo Greco of Bagheria (Sicily), was charged with money laundering. The indictment charged Francesco Polizzi with being an "investor" in and customer of the Catalano/Ganci joint venture. Defendants Baldassare Amato and Cesare Bonventre were charged with being investors in and wholesale distributors for the operation, while Filippo Casamento was accused of being Ganci's wholesale drug customer.

The indictment charged Giovanni Cangiolosi, a representative of the Corleonesi family, with participation in the conspiracy. It alleged that he had been sent to the United States to resolve disputes among the traffickers. . . .

The Trial

Of the thirty-five defendants named in the indictment, only twenty-two appeared for trial; the remainder either had fled, died, been prosecuted in Europe, pled guilty, or entered into cooperation agreements with the government. Of these twenty-two defendants, nineteen remained at the trial's end; Gaetano Mazzara was murdered in December 1986, while Vincenzo Randazzo and Lorenzo DeVardo pled guilty to lesser charges during the course of the trial.

Federal District Judge Pierre Leval presided; Assistant United States Attorneys Louis Freeh, Richard Martin, Robert Stewart, and Robert Bucknam represented the government. Selection of the trial's twenty-four anonymous jurors and alternates took one month; ultimately, the financial and personal hardship of serving on a seventeen-month trial whittled their number to sixteen.

Before trial, the defendants moved to sever the prosecution into several smaller conspiracy cases. Judge Leval ruled that with the exception of one defendant, the government's indictment properly charged a single drug importation and RICO conspiracy. The result was a trial of staggering complexity for jurors and lawyers alike. It brought the term "megatrial" into American jurisprudence and sparked a debate on the fairness of such prosecutions.

Four rows of seating in the fifth-floor courtroom at the Southern District's Foley Square courthouse were converted into seating for the defendants and their attorneys. The courtroom had to be wired for simultaneous Italian translation. The trial also required three translators and a host of United States marshalls for security.

The Southern District had seen large RICO prosecutions before, but *Badalamenti* was Foley Square's longest criminal trial. It generated over forty thousand pages of transcript and occupied dozens of lawyers for the three years between indictment and verdict. The twenty opening defense statements urged differing and often contradictory interpretations of the case's complex facts upon the jury. The trial was similarly marked by multiple cross-examinations, motions, objections, and affirmative defenses from the disparate defense team. The jurors faced the Herculean challenge of compartmentalizing the evidence against each of the defendants whose roles we sketched briefly above.

Two dramatic incidents during the trial exacerbated the conflicts within the defense camp. The murder of Gaetano Mazzara in December 1986, and the shooting of Pietro Alfano in February 1987, both sparked speculation by journalists and law enforcement officials of conflict among the defendants. It was widely theorized that Mazzara's murder, which occurred the weekend before his defense was to begin, was ordered by codefendants afraid that he would implicate them. After the Alfano shooting, the Badalamenti family members requested that they be placed in protective custody. This caused tensions between the Catalano and Badalamenti defendants to rise to the point that Ivan Fisher, attorney for Salvatore Catalano, felt compelled to publicly deny that his client was involved in the Alfano shooting. . . .

The Verdict and Sentencing

The jury retired to begin deliberations on February 25, 1987, accompanied by the one hundred and twenty-page indictment, three hundred and fifty pages of charges and instructions, four hundred and ten pages of evidentiary charts and summaries prepared by the government, and the fifty-nine-page verdict sheet. The jury took only six days to arrive at its verdicts. Vito Badalamenti, Gaetano's son, was the only defendant acquitted of all charges. Fifteen defendants were convicted of all charges. Mazzurco and Salvatore Lamberti were convicted of drug trafficking and RICO conspiracies but cleared of the continuing criminal enterprise charges. Salamone was found not guilty of the RICO and narcotics conspiracy charges but was convicted of currency-reporting violations.

Judge Leval sentenced ten of the defendants to between twenty and thirty-five years, five to between twelve and fifteen years, and four to five years or less. He also imposed significant fines, including $125,000 for Badalamenti and $1.15 million for Salvatore Catalano. In addition, in a novel application of the Victim and Witness Protection Act, Judge Leval ordered eight defendants collectively to pay $3.3 million to a fund for the rehabilitation of drug addicts.

The Appeal

Fifteen of the eighteen convicted defendants appealed their convictions. The Second Circuit's consolidated opinion, *United States v. Casamento* [(1989)], addressed ten of the appellants' arguments in detail. With the exception of the sufficiency of evidence appeals, on which Giuseppe Trupiano's convictions were completely overturned and Frank Castronovo's continuing criminal enterprise conviction was overturned, the court found that Judge Leval had either been correct in his rulings or had made harmless errors. Three of the Second Circuit's holdings will be examined below.

The Atmosphere and Size of the Trial. The appellants argued that the courtroom atmosphere created by the mass joinder, by the media attention it attracted, and by the violence that occurred during the proceedings made a fair trial impossible. Rejecting this argument, the Second Circuit wrote, "We will presume the jury followed [Judge Leval's] admonitions and avoided exposure to news reports about the trial," and, in evaluation of the trial's violence, "Whether the sudden absences of [Gaetano] Mazzara and [Pietro] Alfano from the courtroom may possibly have made the jury more inclined to believe that these two defendants, and by association, the rest of the defendants, led lives of violence is a matter of conjecture."

The court further rejected the argument that the trial was so long and complex that the jurors, unable to assimilate the evidence, had no alternative but to rely uncritically on the government's summary book and charts. Despite the fact that the jurors reached their verdicts in only six days, the court found that the handful of not-guilty verdicts demonstrated the jury's ability to evaluate critically the evidence against each defendant.

Further, the court determined that a "lengthy, multi-defendant narcotics conspiracy trial [is] not beyond the ken of the ordinary, juror, since [the] purchase and sale of hard drugs is basically a simple operation." Finally, the court found that the not-guilty verdicts disposed of the appellants' argument that spillover prejudice had tainted the jury results; if the jury could distinguish those charges where it failed to find guilt, this implied that its evaluations of each charge were unaffected by its analyses of the other charges.

Further, the court rejected the argument that conflicts among the defendants had exacerbated the spillover prejudice, concluding that "severance is not necessarily warranted even if the defendants are hostile or attempt to cast the blame on each other." The court concluded, "Differences [in trial strategies] will almost inevitably occur in multi-defendant trials, and to hold that they require severance would effectively ban this type of trial; we decline to impose such a ban."

Though the appellate panel declined to impose a ban on mass trials, it did set out guidelines to control the size of future trials. In the future, where the trial judge determines that the time for presentation of the government's case will exceed four months, the prosecutor must file a motion demonstrating that a joint trial is more conducive to a fair administration of justice than a series of smaller trials; in cases with more than ten defendants, the government's burden of justification is particularly heavy. The court's discussion concluded with a plea:

> [T]he judge is to be commended for the fairness, patience, and sound judgement he displayed throughout the conduct of this most extraordinary proceeding. Nevertheless, we offer the guidance outlined in the preceding paragraphs in the hope that we will not soon be again presented with the transcript of a seventeen month trial in which more than thirty persons were named as defendants.

Sufficiency of Evidence. The sufficiency-of-evidence appeals achieved some success. Defendant Giuseppe Trupiano's convictions were completely overturned; the court held that the government's sole evidence against him, a conversation in which he considered Alfano's request to "take a walk" if Alfano could send his "daughter or someone to stay with my wife," was legally insufficient to prove beyond a reasonable doubt that Trupiano was aware of and participated in the conspiracy. The court also overturned Castronovo's conviction on the continuing criminal enterprise charge, holding that the evidence did not show that he had controlled the activities of five other members of the conspiracy.

The Restitution Penalties. The appellants' sole other success lay in the Second Circuit's overturning of the restitution penalties imposed on eight defendants. The court concluded that the Victim and Witness Protection Act limited restitution orders to victims whose damages could be attributed directly to actions of specific defendants. Consequently, defendants in drug cases could not be ordered to pay restitution to drug rehabilitation centers that serve the general public.

The Significance of *Badalamenti*

Ultimately, *Badalamenti* was most significant for laying to rest the longstanding debate over Cosa Nostra's involvement with drug trafficking, for demonstrating the drug-smuggling alliance between the Sicilian and American organized crime families, and for illustrating the international scope of their operations. Students of Cosa Nostra and even former family members turned state's witnesses have time and again recounted the injunction against drug dealing. For example, former Los Angeles family underboss Jimmy Fratiano testified that the drug-dealing ban is one of the Cosa Nostra rules whose violation is punishable by death. Likewise, in the Commission case, Tommaso Buscetta confirmed the ban on drug dealing; as recently as 1993, Salvatore Gravano repeated this assertion.

It seems likely that differences of opinion about the propriety of trafficking in drugs have caused substantial conflict and disruption within Cost Nostra since the late 1970s. Some observers believe, for example, that the civil war within the Bonanno family was sparked by commission sponsorship of Philip Rastelli, who had committed to shutting down the drug dealing established by boss Carmine Galante. Another theory holds that Paul Castellano was assassinated because he was intent on enforcing the drug ban within the Gambino family by imposing a death sentence upon John Gotti's brother, Gene, and close friend, Angelo Ruggiero.

Organized crime's involvement in drug dealing merits extensive study. If there is a Cost Nostra ban on drugs, it clearly has been frequently violated over many years. In 1986, the President's Commission on Organized Crime concluded that drug dealing is the norm rather than the exception in the contemporary Mafia. *Badalamenti* lends support to this conclusion.

The Pizza Connection case demonstrated the significant developments in the internationalization of both crime and law enforcement that have occurred in recent years. For the first time, the Sicilian Mafia was shown to be active in the United States; more broadly, the prosecution exposed the sort of sophisticated international structure that is required to sustain ongoing, large-scale drug trafficking. The investigation of this United States-Sicilian connection led to the forging of new international cooperation among law enforcement agencies. The investigation was truly multinational: police of three countries—the United States, Switzerland, and Italy—were integral to the operation, the Spanish police cooperated in the final seizure of Badalamenti, and the Turkish police provided United States investigators with background information on the Mediterranean morphine trade.

In monitoring and recording the communications of the *Badalamenti* defendants, these police agencies employed a wide range of sophisticated surveillance tools, such as concealed video cameras, pen registers, eavesdropping devices, and computer-aided telephone tracing systems. The conspirators showed astonishment that their international payphone-to-payphone calls had been tapped. Contemporary Cosa Nostra members must operate under the assumption that their communications are not secure against modern-day, high-tech government eavesdropping.

More than any other case, *Badalamenti* demonstrates how formidable an opponent to organized crime law enforcement has become. Remarkable changes in law enforcement methods, commitments, and technology occurring over the last three decades will make it impossible for organized crime to operate in its traditional way.

CHAPTER 3

Allowing Preventive
Detention of the Accused

Case Overview

United States v. Salerno (1987)

By the time *United States v. Salerno* reached the Supreme Court, much of the original drama of the case had been removed. Previously referred to as "The Commission Trial," the *Salerno* case was instrumental in proving the existence of an extensive organized crime network in New York City. Operated by five families, the Commission was involved in extortion, loan sharking, and murder. When *Salerno* reached the Supreme Court, however, the case had been reduced to fundamental constitutional questions revolving around the Fifth and Eighth Amendments. In 1984, Congress passed the Bail Reform Act, legislation that allowed courts to detain potentially dangerous individuals without bail before trial. Salerno argued that the Bail Reform Act was illegal, and that it violated both due process in the Fifth Amendment and the excessive bail clause in the Eighth Amendment. The Second District Appeals Court agreed that preventive detention was unconstitutional.

Chief Justice William Rehnquist delivered the five to three majority decision for the court, reversing the Appeals Court decision. Rehnquist supported the majority's decision with two broad arguments, the first addressing due process and the second addressing the excessive bail clause. In essence, he argued that preventive detention as outlined in Bail Reform Act of 1984 was permissible because it included safeguards (allowing, for instance, the accused to call witnesses and provide testimony in his or her defense) and because Congress had not intended pretrial detention as punishment. In fact, pretrial detention was designed to protect a community from the potential threat of a dangerous person awaiting trial. In the majority's argument addressing excessive bail, the court expressed the belief that while the Eighth Amendment addressed excessive bail, the amendment never stated that bail could not be denied. Traditionally, bail had been denied in certain types of cases, such as capital crimes. As it pertained to the Fifth and Eighth Amendments, then, the Bail Reform Act of 1984 was constitutional.

Three associate justices offered vigorous dissents in the case, the most detailed being written by Associate Justice Thurgood Marshall joined by Associate Justice William J. Brennan. The dissent argued that congressional intentions in regard to the Bail Reform Act of 1984 failed to support the idea that preventive detention was not punishment. In fact, he argued, holding anyone because he or she *might* commit a crime denies this person due process under the Fifth Amendment, labeling him or her as guilty before trial. Likewise, Marshall argued that the majority's reasoning in regard to the excessive bail clause was equally faulty. In fact, if the courts can ignore the excessive bail clause in the Eighth Amendment, then there was no reason to pass the Bail Reform Act. Because it violates precepts in the Fifth and Eighth Amendments, preventive detention, as set forth under the Bail Reform Act, is unconstitutional.

While the lower court decision in *Salerno* significantly reduced the power of organized crime in New York City, the Supreme Court ruling had far-reaching implications for the rights of those accused of being involved in organized crime. But while the Supreme Court decision ruled that the Bail Reform Act of 1984 was constitutional, the court's decision failed to detail how preventive detention would be enacted in the courtroom. The full impact of the *Salerno* decision, then, played out between law enforcement, lawyers, and judges in numerous cases for years to come.

"We believe that, when Congress has mandated detention on the basis of a compelling interest other than prevention of flight . . . the Eighth Amendment does not require release on bail."

The Court's Decision: Law Enforcement Can Legally Detain Individuals Believed to Be Dangerous Before Trial

William Rehnquist

William Rehnquist was appointed as an associate justice to the Supreme Court by President Richard Nixon in 1972, and appointed as chief justice by President Ronald Reagan in 1986. Rehnquist served as chief justice for nineteen years.

The major question pending in United States v. Salerno *(1987) was whether it was legal to deny bail and detain individuals accused of crimes before trial under the Bail Reform Act of 1984. Chief Justice Rehnquist, answering for the majority, argues that the Bail Reform Act is constitutional on two grounds. First, he maintains that preventive detention is permissible because it is not designed to punish individuals. Evidence for this point of view originates with the legislation itself, he says: Congress did not design preventive detention as punishment, but as a safeguard to protect the public. Furthermore, he points out that individuals awaiting trial are retained separately from convicted criminals, and the Speedy Trial Act guarantees a short detention.*

William Rehnquist, majority opinion, *United States v. Salerno*, May 26, 1987. http://supreme.justia.com.

Secondly, the court determined that while the Eighth Amendment addresses excessive bail, it never states that bail has to be set. Because of these reasons, and because the Bail Reform Act includes procedural safeguards to protect individual rights, the majority concludes that the act is constitutional.

The Bail Reform Act of 1984 allows a federal court to detain an arrestee pending trial if the Government demonstrates by clear and convincing evidence after an adversary hearing that no release conditions "will reasonably assure . . . the safety of any other person and the community." The United States Court of Appeals for the Second Circuit struck down this provision of the Act as facially unconstitutional, because, in that court's words, this type of pretrial detention violates, "substantive due process." We granted certiorari because of a conflict among the Courts of Appeals regarding the validity of the Act. We hold that, as against the facial attack mounted by these respondents, the Act fully comports with constitutional requirements. We therefore reverse.

Responding to "the alarming problem of crimes committed by persons on release," Congress formulated the Bail Reform Act of 1984, as the solution to a bail crisis in the federal courts. The Act represents the National Legislature's considered response to numerous perceived deficiencies in the federal bail process. By providing for sweeping changes in both the way federal courts consider bail applications and the circumstances under which bail is granted, Congress hoped to

> "give the courts adequate authority to make release decisions that give appropriate recognition to the danger a person may pose to others if released."

To this end, §3141(a) of the Act requires a judicial officer to determine whether an arrestee shall be detained. Section 3142(e) provides that

> "[i]f, after a hearing pursuant to the provisions of subsection (f), the judicial officer finds that no condition or com-

bination of conditions will reasonably assure the appearance of the person as required and the safety of any other person and the community, he shall order the detention of the persons prior to trial."

Section 3142(f) provides the arrestee with a number of procedural safeguards. He may request the presence of counsel at the detention hearing, he may testify and present witnesses in his behalf, as well as proffer evidence, and he may cross-examine other witnesses appearing at the hearing. If the judicial officer finds that no conditions of pretrial release can reasonably assure the safety of other persons and the community, he must state his findings of fact in writing, and support his conclusion with "clear and convincing evidence."

The judicial officer is not given unbridled discretion in making the detention determination. Congress has specified the considerations relevant to that decision. These factors include the nature and seriousness of the charges, the substantiality of the Government's evidence against the arrestee, the arrestee's background and characteristics, and the nature and seriousness of the danger posed by the suspect's release. Should a judicial officer order detention, the detainee is entitled to expedited appellate review of the detention order.

The Lower Court and Detention

Respondents Anthony Salerno and Vincent Cafaro were arrested on March 21, 1986, after being charged in a 29-count indictment alleging various Racketeer Influenced and Corrupt Organizations Act (RICO) violations, mail and wire fraud offenses, extortion, and various criminal gambling violations. The RICO counts alleged 35 acts of racketeering activity, including fraud, extortion, gambling, and conspiracy to commit murder. At respondents' arraignment, the Government moved to have Salerno and Cafaro detained on the ground that no condition of release would assure the safety of the community or any person. The District Court held a hearing at which the

Government made a detailed proffer of evidence. The Government's case showed that Salerno was the "boss" of the Genovese crime family of La Cosa Nostra, and that Cafaro was a "captain" in the Genovese family. According to the Government's proffer, based in large part on conversations intercepted by a court-ordered wiretap, the two respondents had participated in wide-ranging conspiracies to aid their illegitimate enterprises through violent means. The Government also offered the testimony of two of its trial witnesses, who would assert that Salerno personally participated in two murder conspiracies. Salerno opposed the motion for detention, challenging the credibility of the Government's witnesses. He offered the testimony of several character witnesses, as well as a letter from his doctor stating that he was suffering from a serious medical condition. Cafaro presented no evidence at the hearing, but instead characterized the wiretap conversations as merely "tough talk."

The District Court granted the Government's detention motion, concluding that the Government had established by clear and convincing evidence that no condition or combination of conditions of release would ensure the safety of the community or any person:

> "The activities of a criminal organization such as the Genovese family do not cease with the arrest of its principals and their release on even the most stringent of bail conditions. The illegal businesses, in place for many years, require constant attention and protection, or they will fail. Under these circumstances, this court recognizes a strong incentive on the part of its leadership to continue business as usual. When business as usual involves threats, beatings, and murder, the present danger such people pose in the community is self-evident."

Respondents appealed, contending that, to the extent that the Bail Reform Act permits pretrial detention on the ground that the arrestee is likely to commit future crimes, it is unconstitutional on its face. Over a dissent, the United States Court of Appeals for the Second Circuit agreed. Although the court agreed that pretrial detention could be imposed if the defendants were likely to intimidate witnesses or otherwise jeopardize the trial process, it found

"§3142(e)'s authorization of pretrial detention [on the ground of future dangerousness] repugnant to the concept of substantive due process, which we believe prohibits the total deprivation of liberty simply as a means of preventing future crimes."

The court concluded that the Government could not, consistent with due process, detain persons who had not been accused of any crime merely because they were thought to present a danger to the community.

It reasoned that our criminal law system holds persons accountable for past actions, not anticipated future actions. Although a court could detain an arrestee who threatened to flee before trial, such detention would be permissible because it would serve the basic objective of a criminal system—bringing the accused to trial. . . .

The Bail Reform Act and Due Process

The Due Process Clause of the Fifth Amendment provides that "No person shall . . . be deprived of life, liberty, or property, without due process of law. . . ." This Court has held that the Due Process Clause protects individuals against two types of government action. So-called "substantive due process" prevents the Government from engaging in conduct that "shocks the conscience," or interferes with rights "implicit in the concept of ordered liberty." When government action depriving a person of life, liberty, or property survives substantive due process scrutiny, it must still be implemented in a fair manner. This requirement has traditionally been referred to as "procedural" due process.

Respondents [Salerno and Cafaro] first argue that the Act violates substantive due process because the pretrial detention it authorizes constitutes impermissible punishment before trial. The Government, however, has never argued that pretrial detention could be upheld if it were "punishment." The Court of Appeals assumed that pretrial detention under the Bail Reform Act is regulatory, not penal, and we agree that it is.

As an initial matter, the mere fact that a person is detained does not inexorably lead to the conclusion that the Government has imposed punishment.

To determine whether a restriction on liberty constitutes impermissible punishment or permissible regulation, we first look to legislative intent. Unless Congress expressly intended to impose punitive restrictions, the punitive/regulatory distinction turns on

> "'whether an alternative purpose to which [the restriction] may rationally be connected is assignable for it, and whether it appears excessive in relation to the alternative purpose assigned [to it].'"

We conclude that the detention imposed by the Act falls on the regulatory side of the dichotomy. The legislative history of the Bail Reform Act clearly indicates that Congress did not formulate the pretrial detention provisions as punishment for dangerous individuals. Congress instead perceived pretrial detention as a potential solution to a pressing societal problem. There is no doubt that preventing danger to the community is a legitimate regulatory goal.

Nor are the incidents of pretrial detention excessive in relation to the regulatory goal Congress sought to achieve. The Bail Reform Act carefully limits the circumstances under which detention may be sought to the most serious of crimes. The arrestee is entitled to a prompt detention hearing, and the maximum length of pretrial detention is limited by the stringent time limitations of the Speedy Trial Act. Moreover, as in

Schall v. Martin (1984) the conditions of confinement envisioned by the Act "appear to reflect the regulatory purposes relied upon by the" Government.

As in *Schall*, the statute at issue here requires that detainees be housed in a "facility separate, to the extent practicable, from persons awaiting or serving sentences or being held in custody pending appeal." We conclude, therefore, that the pretrial detention contemplated by the Bail Reform Act is regulatory in nature, and does not constitute punishment before trial in violation of the Due Process Clause. . . .

Bail Reform and the Excessive Bail Clause

Respondents also contend that the Bail Reform Act violates the Excessive Bail Clause of the Eighth Amendment. The Court of Appeals did not address this issue, because it found that the Act violates the Due Process Clause. We think that the Act survives a challenge founded upon the Eighth Amendment.

The Eighth Amendment addresses pretrial release by providing merely that "[e]xcessive bail shall not be required." This Clause, of course, says nothing about whether bail shall be available at all. Respondents nevertheless contend that this Clause grants them a right to bail calculated solely upon considerations of flight. They rely on *Stack v. Boyle* (1951), in which the Court stated that

> "[b]ail set at a figure higher than an amount reasonably calculated [to ensure the defendant's presence at trial] is 'excessive' under the Eighth Amendment."

In respondents' view, since the Bail Reform Act allows a court essentially to set bail at an infinite amount for reasons not related to the risk of flight, it violates the Excessive Bail Clause. Respondents concede that the right to bail they have discovered in the Eighth Amendment is not absolute. A court may, for example, refuse bail in capital cases. And, as the Court of Appeals noted and respondents admit, a court may refuse bail when the defendant presents a threat to the judicial process by intimidating witnesses. Respondents characterize these exceptions as consistent with what they claim to be the sole purpose of bail—to ensure the integrity of the judicial process.

While we agree that a primary function of bail is to safeguard the courts' role in adjudicating the guilt or innocence of defendants, we reject the proposition that the Eighth Amendment categorically prohibits the Government from pursuing other admittedly compelling interests through regulation of pretrial release. The above-quoted dictum in *Stack v. Boyle* is far too slender a reed on which to rest this argument. The Court in *Stack* had no occasion to consider whether the Excessive Bail Clause requires courts to admit all defendants to bail, because the statute before the Court in that case in fact allowed the defendants to be bailed. Thus, the Court had to determine only whether bail, admittedly available in that case, was excessive if set at a sum greater than that necessary to ensure the arrestees' presence at trial.

The holding of *Stack* is illuminated by the Court's holding just four months later in *Carlson v. Landon* (1952). In that case, remarkably similar to the present action, the detainees had been arrested and held without bail pending a determination of deportability. The Attorney General refused to release the individuals,

> "on the ground that there was reasonable cause to believe that [their] release would be prejudicial to the public interest and *would endanger the welfare and safety of the United States.*"

The detainees brought the same challenge that respondents bring to us today: the Eighth Amendment required them to be admitted to bail. The Court squarely rejected this proposition:

> "The Bail Clause was lifted with slight changes from the English Bill of Rights Act. In England, that clause has never

been thought to accord a right to bail in all cases, but merely to provide that bail shall not be excessive in those cases where it is proper to grant bail. When this clause was carried over into our Bill of Rights, nothing was said that indicated any different concept. The Eighth Amendment has not prevented Congress from defining the classes of cases in which bail shall be allowed in this country. Thus, in criminal cases, bail is not compulsory where the punishment may be death. Indeed, the very language of the Amendment fails to say all arrests must be bailable."

Carlson v. Landon was a civil case, and we need not decide today whether the Excessive Bail Clause speaks at all to Congress' power to define the classes of criminal arrestees who shall be admitted to bail. For even if we were to conclude that the Eighth Amendment imposes some substantive limitations on the National Legislature's powers in this area, we would still hold that the Bail Reform Act is valid. Nothing in the text of the Bail Clause limits permissible Government considerations solely to questions of flight. The only arguable substantive limitation of the Bail Clause is that the Government's proposed conditions of release or detention not be "excessive" in light of the perceived evil. Of course, to determine whether the Government's response is excessive, we must compare that response against the interest the Government seeks to protect by means of that response. Thus, when the Government has admitted that its only interest is in preventing flight, bail must be set by a court at a sum designed to ensure that goal, and no more. We believe that, when Congress has mandated detention on the basis of a compelling interest other than prevention of flight, as it has here, the Eighth Amendment does not require release on bail.

In our society, liberty is the norm, and detention prior to trial or without trial is the carefully limited exception. We hold that the provisions for pretrial detention in the Bail Reform Act of 1984 fall within that carefully limited exception. The Act authorizes the detention prior to trial of arrestees charged with serious felonies who are found after an adversary hearing to pose a threat to the safety of individuals or to the community which no condition of release can dispel. The numerous procedural safeguards detailed above must attend this adversary hearing. We are unwilling to say that this congressional determination, based as it is upon that primary concern of every government—a concern for the safety and indeed the lives of citizens—on its face violates either the Due Process Clause of the Fifth Amendment or the Excessive Bail Clause of the Eighth Amendment.

The judgment of the Court of Appeals is therefore *Reversed.*

"Our fundamental principles of justice
declare that the defendant is as innocent on the day before his trial as he is
on the morning after his acquittal."

Dissenting Opinion: Detaining Individuals Before Trial Violates the Constitution

Thurgood Marshall

*Justice Thurgood Marshall was the first African-American asso-
ciate justice of the Supreme Court. He was nominated by President Lyndon Johnson in 1967 and retired from the court in
1991.*

*In a dissenting opinion, Justice Thurgood Marshall rejects the
reasoning of the majority: That the Bail Reform Act, which permitted pretrial detention without bail, is constitutional. In regard to pretrial detention, he says, that while the court may state
that pretrial detention is "regulatory" (for the safety of the
community) and not punitive, imprisoning someone without
trial is nonetheless punishment. In addition, arguing that the
Excessive Bail Clause in the Eight Amendment does not guarantee the constitutional right of bail is disingenuous, he maintains
that if the courts do not need to offer bail, then the Bail Reform
Act itself is unnecessary. Marshall finds that both preventive detention and the refusal of bail run counter to the Fifth and
Eighth Amendments of the Bill of Rights, and counter to the presumption that one is innocent until one has been tried and convicted in a court of law.*

Thurgood Marshall, dissenting opinion, *United States v. Salerno*, May 26, 1987. http://
supreme.justia.com.

This case brings before the Court for the first time a statute in which Congress declares that a person innocent of any crime may be jailed indefinitely, pending the trial of allegations which are legally presumed to be untrue, if the Government shows to the satisfaction of a judge that the accused is likely to commit crimes, unrelated to the pending charges, at any time in the future. Such statutes, consistent with the usages of tyranny and the excesses of what bitter experience teaches us to call the police state, have long been thought incompatible with the fundamental human rights protected by our Constitution. Today a majority of this Court holds otherwise. Its decision disregards basic principle of justice established centuries ago and enshrined beyond the reach of governmental interference in the Bill of Rights. . . .

Pretrial Detention Is Punishment

The majority approaches respondents' challenge to the Act by dividing the discussion into two sections, one concerned with the substantive guarantees implicit in the Due Process Clause and the other concerned with the protection afforded by the Excessive Bail Clause of the Eighth Amendment. This is a sterile formalism, which divides a unitary argument into two independent parts and then professes to demonstrate that the parts are individually inadequate.

On the due process side of this false dichotomy appears an argument concerning the distinction between regulatory and punitive legislation. The majority concludes that the Act is a regulatory, rather than a punitive, measure. The ease with which the conclusion is reached suggests the worthlessness of the achievement. The major premise is that

"[u]nless Congress expressly intended to impose punitive restrictions, the punitive/regulatory distinction turns on *'whether an alternative purpose to which [the restriction] may rationally be connected is assignable for it, and whether it appears excessive in relation to the alternative purpose assigned [to it]."*

The majority finds that "Congress did not formulate the pretrial detention provisions as punishment for dangerous individuals" but instead was pursuing the "legitimate regulatory goal" of "preventing danger to the community." Concluding that pretrial detention is not an excessive solution to the problem of preventing danger to the community, the majority thus finds that no substantive element of the guarantee of due process invalidates the statute.

This argument does not demonstrate the conclusion it purports to justify. Let us apply the majority's reasoning to a similar, hypothetical case. After investigation, Congress determines (not unrealistically) that a large proportion of violent crime is perpetrated by persons who are unemployed. It also determines, equally reasonably, that much violent crime is committed at night. From amongst the panoply of "potential solutions," Congress chooses a statute which permits, after judicial proceedings, the imposition of a dusk-to-dawn curfew on anyone who is unemployed. Since this is not a measure enacted for the purpose of punishing the unemployed, and since the majority finds that preventing danger to the community is a legitimate regulatory goal, the curfew statute would, according to the majority's analysis, be a mere "regulatory" detention statute, entirely compatible with the substantive components of the Due Process Clause.

The absurdity of this conclusion arises, of course, from the majority's cramped concept of substantive due process. The majority proceeds as though the only substantive right protected by the Due Process Clause is a right to be free from punishment before conviction. The majority's technique for infringing this right is simple: merely redefine any measure which is claimed to be punishment as "regulation," and, magically, the Constitution no longer prohibits its imposition.

Because . . . the Due Process Clause protects other substantive rights which are infringed by this legislation, the majority's argument is merely an exercise in obfuscation.

Preventive Detention Is Unconstitutional

The logic of the majority's Eighth Amendment analysis is equally unsatisfactory. The Eighth Amendment, as the majority notes, states that "[e]xcessive bail shall not be required." The majority then declares, as if it were undeniable, that: "[t]his Clause, of course, says nothing about whether bail shall be available at all." If excessive bail is imposed, the defendant stays in jail. The same result is achieved if bail is denied altogether. Whether the magistrate sets bail at $1 billion or refuses to set bail at all, the consequences are indistinguishable. It would be mere sophistry to suggest that the Eighth Amendment protects against the former decision, and not the latter. Indeed, such a result would lead to the conclusion that there was no need for Congress to pass a preventive detention measure of any kind; every federal magistrate and district judge could simply refuse, despite the absence of any evidence of risk of flight or danger to the community, to set bail. This would be entirely constitutional, since, according to the majority, the Eighth Amendment "says nothing about whether bail shall be available at all."

But perhaps, the majority says, this manifest absurdity can be avoided. Perhaps the Bail Clause is addressed only to the Judiciary. "[W]e need not decide today," the majority says, "whether the Excessive Bail Clause speaks at all to Congress' power to define the classes of criminal arrestees who shall be admitted to bail."

The majority is correct that this question need not be decided today: it was decided long ago. Federal and state statutes which purport to accomplish what the Eighth Amendment forbids, such as imposing cruel and unusual punishments, may not stand. The text of the Amendment, which provides simply that "[e]xcessive bail shall not be required, nor excessive fines imposed, nor cruel and unusual punishments inflicted," provides absolutely no support for the majority's speculation that both courts and Congress are forbidden to inflict cruel and unusual punishments, while only the courts are forbidden to require excessive bail.

The majority's attempts to deny the relevance of the Bail Clause to this case are unavailing, but the majority is nonetheless correct that the prohibition of excessive bail means that, in order "to determine whether the Government's response is excessive, we must compare that response against the interest the Government seeks to protect by means of that response."

The majority concedes, as it must, that, "when the Government has admitted that its only interest is in preventing flight, bail must be set by a court at a sum designed to ensure that goal, and no more."

But, the majority says, "when Congress has mandated detention on the basis of a compelling interest other than prevention of flight, as it has here, the Eighth Amendment does not require release on bail."

This conclusion follows only if the "compelling" interest upon which Congress acted is an interest which the Constitution permits Congress to further through the denial of bail. The majority does not ask, as a result of its disingenuous division of the analysis, if there are any substantive limits contained in both the Eighth Amendment and the Due Process Clause which render this system of preventive detention unconstitutional. The majority does not ask, because the answer is apparent and, to the majority, inconvenient. . . .

The majority's untenable conclusion that the present Act is constitutional arises from a specious denial of the role of the Bail Clause and the Due Process Clause in protecting the invaluable guarantee afforded by the presumption of innocence. "The principle that there is a presumption of innocence in favor of the accused is the undoubted law, axiomatic and elementary, and its enforcement lies at the foundation of the administration of our criminal law."

"Our society's belief, reinforced over the centuries, that all are innocent until the state has proved them to be guilty, like the companion principle that guilt must be proved beyond a reasonable doubt, is "implicit in the concept of ordered liberty," and is established beyond legislative contravention in the Due Process Clause.

The statute now before us declares that persons who have been indicted may be detained if a judicial officer finds clear and convincing evidence that they pose a danger to individuals or to the community. The statute does not authorize the Government to imprison anyone it has evidence is dangerous; indictment is necessary. But let us suppose that a defendant is indicted and the Government shows by clear and convincing evidence that he is dangerous and should be detained pending a trial, at which trial the defendant is acquitted. May the Government continue to hold the defendant in detention based upon its showing that he is dangerous? The answer cannot be yes, for that would allow the Government to imprison someone for uncommitted crimes based upon "proof" not beyond a reasonable doubt. The result must therefore be that, once the indictment has failed, detention cannot continue. But our fundamental principles of justice declare that the defendant is as innocent on the day before his trial as he is on the morning after his acquittal. Under this statute, an untried indictment somehow acts to permit a detention, based on other charges, which after an acquittal would be unconstitutional. The conclusion is inescapable that the indictment has been turned into evidence, if not that the defendant is guilty of the crime charged, then that, left to his own devices, he will soon be guilty of something else."

"In the federal court system liberty is not the norm; in fact, detention is the norm for accused persons awaiting trial."

Preventive Detention Hurts Pretrial Justice

Marie VanNostrand and Gena Keebler

Marie VanNostrand is a senior consultant at Luminosity, Inc., a contributor to Federal Probation, *and the author of "Legal and Evidence Based Practices: Application of Legal Principles, Laws, and Research to the Field of Pretrial Services." Gena Keebler is the president of Luminosity, Inc. and a contributor to* Federal Probation.

In the majority opinion for the case United States v. Salerno *(1987), which upheld preventive detention, Chief Justice Rehnquist wrote: "In our society, liberty is the norm, and detention . . . is the carefully limited exception." Using data that includes pretrial release and detention rates, Marie VanNostrand and Gena Keebler show that our country has not followed Chief Justice Rehnquist's assertion. In fact, the country may have replaced pretrial justice with preventive detention.*

In order to effectively assess our progress in achieving pretrial justice, it is critical to understand the pretrial stage of the criminal justice system, including the bail decision, the rights of accused persons awaiting trial, and the role of pretrial services. We will begin with a review of the basics. The

Marie VanNostrand, and Gena Keebler, "Our Journey Toward Pretrial Justice," *Federal Probation*, September 2007. Reproduced by permission.

period of time between arrest and case adjudication is known as the pretrial stage. Each time a person is arrested and accused of a crime, a decision must be made as to whether the accused person, known as the defendant, will be released back into the community or detained in jail awaiting trial. A critical part of the pretrial stage is the bail decision—the decision to release or detain a defendant pending trial and the setting of terms and conditions of bail. The bail decision is a reflection of pretrial justice; it is the primary attempt to balance the rights afforded to accused persons awaiting trial with the need to protect the community, maintain the integrity of the judicial process, and assure court appearance.

To begin the discussion of measuring our progress toward pretrial justice, we chose a measurement that reflects many of the components of pretrial justice. We examine our progress toward pretrial justice by assessing whether or not our system operates as Chief Justice Rehnquist wrote for the majority in *United States v. Salerno* in 1987: "In our society, liberty is the norm, and detention prior to trial or without trial is the carefully limited exception." It is important to recognize that this case was decided after the Bail Reform Acts of 1966 and 1984 and, in fact, upheld the challenge to the preventive detention aspect of the 1984 Act. For this reason, this statement provides an appropriate measure of pretrial justice today and the results will serve as a reflection of our progress toward pretrial justice. Examining pretrial release and detention rates as well as the population of our jails in this country is a reliable way of determining whether liberty is the norm and detention awaiting trial the carefully limited exception.

Release and Detention Rates in U.S. District Courts

The United States district courts are the trial courts of the federal court system. There are 94 federal judicial districts, including at least one district in each state, the District of Columbia and Puerto Rico. In addition, three territories of the United States (Virgin Islands, Guam, and the Northern Mariana Islands) have district courts that hear federal cases.

An examination of the 2006 annual report reveals that the U.S. district courts handled 82,508 cases (defendants) during the 12-month period ending September 30, 2006. Of those cases, 39 percent of the defendants were released at some point awaiting trial. Conversely, 61 percent of all defendants were detained during the entire pretrial stage. It should be noted that rates varied by circuit and district in the U.S., excluding U.S. territories, and ranged from a high of 74.5 percent released in Vermont to a low of 11.2 percent released in Arizona. During fiscal year 2006 the Administrative Office of the U.S. Courts reported these statistics excluding immigration cases for the first time. When excluding immigration cases the release rate for all courts increased to 47.3 percent, with release rates ranging from a high of 76.3 percent in Vermont to a low of 23.8 percent in the Southern District of California. Even after removing the immigration cases, the average detention rate in all U.S. district courts during fiscal year 2006 was over 50 percent.

Release and detention data for the U.S. district courts from fiscal years 1992 to 2006 provided by the Administrative Office of the U.S. Courts were analyzed to identify trends in these rates over the past 15 years.

Release rates have gradually decreased over the past 15 years, while detention rates have increased. In fact, defendants released awaiting trial averaged a high of 62 percent in 1992 and decreased to a low of 39 percent by 2006.

U.S. Jail Populations

In addition to release and detention rates in the federal and state court systems, it is interesting to consider the make-up of jails in this country when assessing our progress toward pretrial justice. Jails are locally operated correctional facilities that confine persons before or after case adjudication. Accused persons awaiting trial and offenders sentenced to usually one year or less are incarcerated in jails. According to the Bureau of Justice Statistics, as of midyear 2005 there were nearly 750,000 persons incarcerated in local jails on an average day in this country, and of those, 62 percent are defendants being detained pending trial. An analysis of the jail populations for the 10 years between 1996 and 2005 reveals an increase in the percent of the population awaiting trial from 51 percent in 1996 to 62 percent in 2005.

Do We Really Have Pretrial Justice?

Liberty pending trial equates to pretrial release. In the federal court system in FY2006 the pretrial release rate was 39 percent including immigration cases and 47 percent when excluding them. The pretrial release rate in the federal court system is at an all-time low—down from 62 percent in 1992. The most recent state court statistics from 2002 show a 62 percent release rate for felony defendants in the 75 most populous counties in the U.S., while nearly two-thirds of our local jails on an average day in this country are filled with accused persons awaiting trial—over 450,000.

In the federal court system liberty is not the norm; in fact, detention is the norm for accused persons awaiting trial (61 percent detained). In the state court system detention prior to trial or without trial is not the carefully limited exception (38 percent detained, with nearly two-thirds of our local jails consisting of accused persons awaiting trial). After considering federal and state court system data from the past 10 to 15 years we must conclude that in our society liberty is not the norm and detention prior to trial or without trial is not the carefully limited exception. It must also be acknowledged that we have veered further and further away from the achievement of pretrial justice as measured by the statement provided by Chief Justice Rehnquist. It is disheartening yet fair to say that we, as a society and a criminal justice system, have lost our way along the path toward pretrial justice.

Some Commentators Disagree with *Salerno*

Stanislaw Frankowski

Stanislaw Frankowski teaches at the St. Louis University School of Law and has authored numerous books focusing on criminal law.

In United States v. Salerno *(1987), the Supreme Court attempted to settle the constitutionality of the 1984 Bail Reform Act. The Supreme Court upheld the constitutionality of the act, but according to Stanislaw Frankowski, many critics believed the court relied on weak legal reasoning.*

Originally, a Second District Federal Court had detained Salerno, arguing that he posed a threat to the community if released; the Second District Appeals Court, however, reversed this decision. The Supreme Court backed the original decision, arguing that the Bail Reform Act allowed detention and that detention, even before a trial, did not qualify as punishment. Many critics question the Supreme Court's legal reasoning, however, Frankowski points to legal scholars who have argued that being locked in a federal prison with potentially dangerous criminals and overcrowding is punishment, and furthermore, notes that there are cases where detainees have been held over a year before

Stanislaw Frankowski, "Stanislaw Frankowski and Henry Luepke: Pre-trial Detention in the U.S.," *Preventive Detention: A Comparative and International Law Perspective.* Dordrecht: Martinus Nijhoff Publishers, 1992, pp. 84–93. Copyright © 1992 Kluwer Academic Publishers. Reproduced with kind permission from Springer Science and Business Media and the author.

trial. He notes that the Supreme Court also rejected Salerno's argument that the Eighth Amendment guarantees the right of bail, though once again, most commentators believe that historically, the Eighth Amendment has guaranteed this right.

From its inception, the 1984 Act [Bail Reform Act] has come under heavy constitutional attack. Such criticism continues even after the U.S. Supreme Court's decision in *United States v. Salerno*. In *Salerno*, Anthony ('Fat Tony') Salerno, an alleged leader of the Genovese crime family of La Cosa Nostra, was charged with a twenty-nine count indictment for Racketeer Influenced and Corrupt Organizations Act (RICO) violations. These charges included mail and wire fraud, extortion, gambling violations and conspiracies to commit murder. When the prosecution moved to detain Salerno pursuant to the 1984 Act, the suspect objected by claiming that the Act was facially unconstitutional under both the Fifth and Eighth Amendments.

The prosecution did not contend in its detention motion that Salerno posed a risk of flight, but instead claimed he was so dangerous that no possible combination of release conditions could assure the safety of the community. At the detention hearing the prosecution offered prospective testimony of witnesses that Salerno 'could order a murder merely by voicing his assent with the single word "hit"'. The court found this allegation sufficient to support a finding that the defendant was dangerous and therefore should be detained. The presiding judge rejected his arguments for conditional release because both the seriousness of the alleged crimes 'and the ease with which they could be ordered weigh heavily in favor of finding that Salerno is a present danger to the community'.

The defendant appealed the detention order to the Second Circuit Court of Appeals, which ruled that pretrial detention as a means of preventing future crime violated due process as protected by the Fifth Amendment. Thereafter, the prosecution appealed the case to the U.S. Supreme Court which reversed the Second Circuit decision and upheld the constitutionality of the 1984 Act. Chief Justice [William] Rehnquist, writing for the majority, first dealt with Salerno's Fifth Amendment substantive due process challenge. As interpreted by the U.S. Supreme Court, the due process clause protects individuals against government action which violates either procedural or substantive due process. In particular, the Fifth Amendment due process clause protects an accused against punishment until the prosecution proves, beyond a reasonable doubt, and in a manner provided by law, every fact necessary to constitute the crime charged. In challenging the Act, Salerno argued that his preventive detention amounted to punishment before adjudication of guilt. Thus, according to the defendant, the Act's preventive detention violated the Fifth Amendment's presumption of innocence.

Preventive Detention: Regulatory or Punitive?

The Court rejected this argument by characterizing the Act's preventive detention as regulatory instead of punitive. In deciding that the statute was regulatory and not punitive, the Court relied primarily, if not exclusively, on the legislative intent of the Act. 'Unless Congress expressly intended to impose punitive restrictions, the punitive/regulatory distinction turns on "whether an alternative purpose to which [the restriction] may rationally be connected is assignable for it, and whether it appears excessive in relation to the alternative purpose assigned [to it]"'. Since Congress did not indicate a punitive intent, the Court weighed the alternative state purpose of protecting the community, based on the predictive finding of dangerousness, against the accused's interest in avoiding detention. The Court found that the preventive detention was not excessive in relation to the goal pursued by the government in protecting the community, and concluded that the Act's preventive detention was regulatory rather than punitive.

Further, in determining that the preventive detention was not punitive, the majority pointed out that the 'conditions of confinement envisioned by the Act appear to reflect the regulatory purpose relied upon by the government'. The Court noted in particular that the Act requires detainees to be kept separate, 'to the extent practicable,' from convicted persons. Also, 'the maximum length of detention is limited by the stringent time limitations of the Speedy Trial Act'.

Nevertheless, most analysts contend that in everyday operation the Act's terms are not as protective as the Court assumed. For instance, conditions for detainees are often worse than those for convicted persons. 'Pretrial detainees are often not incarcerated separately from convicted prisoners. In the Metropolitan Correctional Center in Manhattan, where Salerno ... [was] detained, convicts, witnesses in protective custody, and individuals incarcerated for contempt comprise 40–60 percent of the population'. In 1987, jails housed detainees together with 12,361 long-term convicted prisoners, due to overcrowding in state prisons.

Detainees not only endure the excessive overcrowding in jails, but also endure all the other burdens of confinement, such as highly intrusive body searches, jail violence, and rigorous prohibitions on the receipt of packages containing food and personal items from outside the institution. Such severe conditions are partially reflected by the suicide rate of jailed detainees. In 1986, for example, there were 401 suicides in jails, of which 88.7 percent were committed by detainees. In light of these facts, the Court's characterization of pretrial detention as non-punitive seems questionable.

Furthermore, many critics point out that the Court was overly optimistic in relying as it did on the Speedy Trial Act of 1974. Even though the time limitations of the Speedy Trial Act require commencement of trial no later than ninety days after the accused's indictment, they are far from stringent because the Act lists a number of exclusions which permit uncounted delays, thus extending the ninety-day limit. Most notable among these exclusions is a provision that excludes '[a]ny period of delay resulting from a continuance granted by any judge on his own motion or at the request of the [accused] or his counsel or at the request of the attorney for the Government, if the judge granted such continuance on the basis of his findings that the ends of justice served by taking such action outweigh the best interest of the public and the [accused] in a speedy trial'. These excludable delays have eviscerated the ninety-day limit, often resulting in excessively long pretrial detention. For example, in *United States v. Zannino* [(1985)] the detention lasted sixteen months; and it lasted fourteen months in *United States v. Claudio* [(1986)]. Such long detention periods weaken the *Salerno* conclusion that the preventive detention provisions of the 1984 Act are merely regulatory and not punitive. . . .

The Eighth Amendment

Salerno also claimed that the Act violated his implicit Eighth Amendment right to bail. The Court, however, held that no such constitutional right exists. The majority observed that the Eighth Amendment does not say whether bail shall be available at all, and, furthermore, that the 'excessive bail' clause does not apply to legislative action, but only to judicial action by restricting discretion in setting bail or applying detention. . . . Thus, according to the majority, the bail clause of the Eighth Amendment prohibits the judiciary from imposing excessive bail only in those cases where the legislature has statutorily granted such a right. Absent such a statute, the clause simply does not apply.

Several commentators, disagreeing with the *Salerno* Court's interpretation of the bail clause, argue a constitutional right to bail does exist by pointing to its historical foundation.

CHAPTER 4

Organized Crime Boss on Trial

Case Overview

United States v. John Gotti and Frank Locascio (1992)

When *United States v. John Gotti and Frank Locascio* went to trial in 1992, the federal government had already tried, and failed, to convict Gotti three times for various crimes. In one sense, *United States v. John Gotti and Frank Locascio* was important symbolically. Between 1982 and 1991, the federal government convicted a number of high-profile organized crime figures in New York and New Jersey, the result of an aggressive policy toward organized crime by the Justice Department under President Ronald Reagan's administration. In retrospect, critics argued that Gotti, as the boss of the Gambino family, was far less powerful than his predecessors. Nonetheless, Gotti was a well-known public figure who, because he had evaded conviction, was known as the "Teflon Don." Federal prosecutors believed that convicting Gotti, the public face of organized crime, would prove a symbolic victory, a final blow to an already weakened organization.

In another sense, however, *United States v. John Gotti and Frank Locascio* enfolded several important legal elements that aided prosecutors in future cases against organized crime. Significantly, federal prosecutors asked for, and were granted, the disqualification of Gotti's defense lawyers. Because these lawyers were present during incriminating conversations, they could potentially be called as witnesses against Gotti. This dual role, prosecutors argued, created a conflict of interest: as witnesses, the lawyers might be less forthcoming with self-incriminating evidence. Also central for the prosecution's case was the defection of Gotti's underboss, Salvatore Gravano. As a confidant of Gotti, Gravano was privy to intricate details of the Gambino family's criminal activities. Finally, the jury for the trial was sequestered and remained anonymous, legal maneuvers that removed the members from media access and from the possibility of jury tampering (which had occurred in a previous Gotti trial).

These legal procedures greatly strengthened the federal prosecutor's case, but they were not without controversy. Gotti's lawyer, Bruce Cutler, had been central in defending him in the past, and some believed his removal violated Fourth Amendment rights. Also problematic was Gravano's testimony, which, some critics believed, represented conflicts that were similar to those that had led to the removal of Gotti's lawyers. Since Gravano was receiving immunity for his own crimes, it would be in his best interest to provide the testimony most useful to federal prosecutors. Furthermore, the federal government was working with a witness whose own crimes (including nineteen murders) were extensive, creating an ethical quandary.

For federal prosecutors, however, these maneuvers were justifiable in completing their work against organized crime. The conviction of Gotti in 1992, resulting in a life sentence, was considered a major victory for the Federal Bureau of Investigation (FBI), and the crowning achievement of the Justice Department's aggressive efforts against organized crime during the preceding ten years. Also symbolic was Gravano's defection. Traditionally, high-ranking organized crime figures preferred serving prison sentences to providing evidence. Gravano's defection proved that organized crime no longer had the power to maintain "family" loyalty. Gotti's conviction represented the end of an era for organized crime.

> "With surveillance, turncoats, wiretaps, and advanced electronics . . . , the government has monitored and pursued family members as quickly as they emerge."

Government Works to Eliminate Gambino Crime Family

Larry Neumeister

Larry Neumeister is a journalist for the Associated Press and a contributing writer for The New York Sun.

Ever since Paul Castellano was shot and replaced as head of the Gambino crime family by John Gotti in 1985, the federal government has worked to shut down the family. After three failed attempts, John Gotti was finally convicted in 1992. His son, Junior Gotti, and his brother, Peter Gotti, both had turns running the family and both were eventually jailed: Junior for racketeering and Peter for ordering a hit. The government's efforts have thrown the family's chain of command into disarray, as even more members have been prosecuted and jailed.

Since the 2002 death of a former Gambino boss, John Gotti, the federal government has tried to permanently crush the notorious crime family by prosecuting his brother and son and rounding up scores of Gambino leaders.

The latest attack on the Gambino family—long recognized as the largest of New York City's five traditional Mafia families—begins today, when lawyers deliver opening statements in the racketeering case against John "Junior" Gotti.

The trial is a linchpin in the government's effort to permanently shut down the Gambino family, once a powerhouse in the gambling, loan sharking, labor union, and extortion rackets.

Recent Efforts Lead to Success

The government has taken steady aim with increasing success at the family since the 1985 street shooting by other mobsters of Paul Castellano, who in 1976 succeeded Carlo Gambino as head of the nation's largest Mafia family.

Prosecutors got off to a sputtering start when the elder Gotti won acquittal at three 1980s trials, earning him the nickname the "Teflon Don."

Lately, they've had more success.

With surveillance, turncoats, wiretaps, and advanced electronics that lawyers say let the government turn one suspected mobster into a walking microphone, the government has monitored and pursued family members as quickly as they emerge.

Last year, 32 men were rounded up in a massive prosecution the government says involved a dozen Gambino members, including its newest top leaders, and others with ties to the family's illegal business.

Investigators say they infiltrated the family with an undercover FBI agent who was so well accepted that he was offered membership.

Putting the Old Bosses Away

Even as the government worked to dismantle new leadership, it worked to put away the old bosses.

The continuous prosecutions have resulted in a game of musical chairs among the crime family's hierarchy.

After John Gotti was convicted in 1992, prosecutors say, Junior Gotti stepped into his father's shoes.

When Junior Gotti pleaded guilty in a racketeering case in 1999 and began a five-year prison sentence, his uncle Peter Gotti allegedly took over the crime family.

Now, Junior Gotti is out of prison—and back on trial—while his uncle is in prison.

Junior Gotti says he no longer has anything to do with the mob; the government begs to differ.

Peter Gotti was sentenced last year to 25 years in prison for ordering a hit on Salvatore "Sammy the Bull" Gravano, the once trusted underboss of John Gotti. Gravano admitted involvement in 19 murders and doomed John Gotti's chances at the 1992 trial.

The Next Step

The government was allowed to pursue a second racketeering trial against Junior Gotti because the case involves different crimes.

Prosecutors say the younger Gotti ordered the kidnapping of Guardian Angels founder and radio personality Curtis Sliwa in retaliation for Mr. Sliwa's on-air rants against his father in 1992.

Mr. Sliwa was shot in the botched early-morning attack by two assailants in a cab but escaped out a window to recover and resume his verbal attacks on the Gotti family.

He testified at Gotti's first racketeering trial, which ended last year with a deadlocked jury.

Gotti insists he had nothing to do with the kidnapping, has left the mob and has started a new life. But prosecutors say he continued his ties even after making the claim. If convicted, Gotti could face 30 years in prison. He is out on bail but must remain in home detention.

> "If ... a lawyer learns ... that he ...
> ought to be called as a witness on be-
> half of his client, he shall withdraw
> from ... the trial ..."

The District Court's Decision: Defense Council Cannot Be a Potential Witness

Leo Glasser

Judge Leo Glasser serves the U.S. District Court in the Eastern District of New York. He was nominated by Ronald Reagan on November 23, 1981, and confirmed by the Senate on December 9, 1981. He received his commission on December 10, 1981, and assumed senior status on July 1, 1993.

Before United States v. John Gotti and Frank Locascio *opened in 1992, U.S. prosecutors moved to disqualify Gotti and Locascio's legal council. The U.S. prosecutors argued that the lawyers who represented the defense were on Gotti's payroll, and thus, were answerable to him. They also argued that because the defendant's lawyers had been privy to conversations detailing illegal activities, they could be called as witnesses, creating a conflict of interest. The defense counter-moved to disqualify the assistant United States attorney John Gleeson from prosecuting the trial. They argued that due to a prior incident involving a search warrant issued to Gleeson's wife, Gleeson would be unduly prejudiced in his pursuit of Gotti. Judge Leo Glasser explains his rationale for disqualifying Gotti and Locascio's lawyers and retaining Gleeson.*

Leo Glasser, decision, *United States v. John Gotti and Frank Locascio,* United States District Court for the Eastern District of New York, January 21, 1992, pp. 6–7. [Ruling that disqualified Locascio and Gotti's lawyers.]

The government has moved this court for an order disqualifying George Santangelo from representing any of the defendants in this case at trial. This motion, like the motion previously made to disqualify Gerald Shargel, Bruce Cutler and John Pollok, is based upon the assertion that counsel's continued participation would give rise to conflicts of interest which cannot be waived or remedied save by an order of disqualification. Defendants have cross-moved for an order disqualifying Assistant United States Attorney John Gleeson from prosecuting this case on behalf of the government.

The government predicates its motion on the assertion that [George] Santangelo's "presence at counsel table would needlessly deprive the government of a fair trial, create a conflict of interest that cannot be waived or remedied by measures other than disqualification, and compromise the integrity of these proceedings by fostering an appearance of impropriety."

A review of the government's proffer yields two bases upon which a motion for disqualification may be predicated: 1) that Santangelo is answerable to defendant John Gotti, the alleged leader of the Gambino Family . . . and 2) that Santangelo's presence at this trial would offend the Model Code of Professional Responsibility.

The government contends that Santangelo is "house counsel to the Gambino Family." In addressing the motion, the court shall use the phrase "answerable to Gotti" rather than "house counsel." The difference is purely semantic: in either case, the pernicious effect upon the institutional interest in the rendition of just criminal verdicts is the same, whether Santangelo is the recipient of "benefactor payments" (an allegation not vigorously advanced by the prosecution) or whether he simply answers to Gotti rather than to Locascio.

Evidence of Santangelo's subservience to Gotti would be relevant to establishing that Gotti is the head of an "enterprise" as that term is used in the RICO [Racketeer Influenced and Corrupt Organizations Act] statute. The evidence the government proffers in support of its claim is the testimony it represents will be given by Salvatore Gravano as well as the tape recordings of conversations intercepted through authorized electronic surveillance.

Gravano was one of the four defendants initially named in the indictment, along with Gotti, Locascio, and Thomas Gambino. The indictment charged Gravano with becoming the *consigliere* (counselor) of the Gambino Family following the incarceration of Joseph N. Gallo on May 30, 1989.

Gravano has now chosen to cooperate with the prosecution. The government states that Gravano will testify that shortly after the defendants were arraigned, Gotti told Gravano that he (Gotti) would assign Santangelo to represent either Gravano or Locascio. Such an "assignment" of counsel by Gotti for his co-defendant would clearly be probative of the existence of the charged RICO enterprise.

That it mattered little which defendant Santangelo would represent—that, in effect, the clients were fungible [could be substituted]—may be readily inferred by the jury from excerpts of intercepted conversations in which Gotti is heard to decree that lawyers (both his and others') work within certain parameters prescribed by him, and that their concern must be not only for their ostensible clients but for others in the Gambino Family as well. Gravano will further testify that Gotti's insistence that lawyers representing the Family march in lock-step contributed to his own decision to cooperate with the government. Evidence of Santangelo's eleventh-hour appearance may warrant the jury to believe that Gravano's testimony in this regard rings true. . . .

The Intercepted Conversations

The government contends that there is other evidence from which a jury could readily conclude that a criminal association exists between Santangelo's clients and Gotti, and that

Gotti is the final arbiter of Santangelo's decisions. Accompanying the government's motion is a transcript of a lawfully intercepted conversation from April 18, 1990, among Gotti, Bruce Cutler, and others. . . .

The essence of the relevant portion of the conversation is Gotti's insistence upon knowing about, and ultimately approving of, all legal activity in the case not only on his own behalf, but also on behalf of others. Gotti ordains the response the attorneys must make to government assertions of the existence of a Mafia, a Cosa Nostra, or a Gambino Crime Family: There are to be no concessions, and there is to be no finger-pointing. Cutler acknowledges his compliance with Gotti's edicts in this regard, assuring Gotti that he met with the lawyers "three times to tell them your credo in life. . . . But I made them understand: No concessions, everything is denied, everything is fought down to the wire."

In an elaboration on his "credo," Gotti is heard to suggest to Cutler that "there ain't nothing" on the tapes as far as he is concerned, and "if there is, it's a mystery to me, I know nothing. . . . Maybe . . . talk to myself a little when I'm talking on that tape." After commenting unfavorably about a portion of a brief which he demands to have deleted, Gotti goes on to say:

Yeah, but you see, Bruce, these things I gotta see before we submit. How many times we gotta go through this . . . you know what I mean? How many times we gonna go through this? I don't want nothin' submitted. . . .

During a discussion in which Cutler attempts to explain the "legalese" of a particular brief, Gotti says: "But I don't want it. Since when have I agreed to that?" The conversation then proceeds as follows:

CUTLER: In other words, you and your friends are friends. It's not the Mafia, it's not the Gambino Family, it's not anything. That's what he means, it's not in your language, it's not written strong enough. I agree with it. I agree with you. I agree with you.

GOTTI: Okay, but here's what I'm saying.

CUTLER: It's not a concession.

GOTTI: Listen to me. Anything that's put in on my behalf, I wanna see it first, anyway. Who the f--- is he to take a liberty?

CUTLER: . . . what I told him in the meeting is, John, when you write this, if you ever say anything about anything like the Mafia, whatever the hell it is . . . you say "the government says it," not us say it.

GOTTI: And I say "No!" No matter what the f---ing tape says, I didn't say anything.

CUTLER: I understand that.

GOTTI: That's what I wanna read!

Shortly thereafter, Gotti declares, "I don't want nothin' put in that they send out unless I love it and see it. Wanna see it. I don't give a f--- what anybody else feels."

As the preceding excerpt indicates, Gotti insists on exerting equally absolute control over the submissions of attorneys representing not him but his associates:

GOTTI: I wanna, I wanna see that,—

CUTLER: From now on—

GOTTI:—not gonna be one word in that I don't see.

CUTLER: You got it, John.

GOTTI: You understand?

CUTLER: You got it, you got it.

GOTTI: And that goes for either George and them, you know what I mean. I'm involved in this. . . .

In discussing Gotti's obdurate insistence upon seeing all submissions, Cutler advises Gotti that he hasn't yet seen a particular brief by Santangelo. When Gotti upbraids Cutler for this oversight, the following exchange ensues:

CUTLER: . . . But with George, Johnny, it's different. With George Santangelo, I never even have to worry. I bet there's not even the slightest iota of a phrase like he says, you understand. With George, I mean, with John Pollok, I have to be more vigilant, and you're a thousand percent right. And I will. . . .

GOTTI: You tell them anything with my f---ing meter—

CUTLER: I will.

GOTTI:—or anything that touches me even in perimeter, I wanna see it first.

CUTLER: John, and I'm, and I'm not putting George in this category because George is not that way. But a majority of these lawyers, who you look at, are known as erudite, professorial, ah, egghead types. Will not put in the brief words to the effect "Go f--- yourself!" I know you can't do that. But they will not put in a brief "and we dispute the existence of the Mafia." I say it all the time. They won't write it down, they just won't write it down.

GOTTI: So don't let them do our work then. Don't do my f--- work!

Gotti's adamant stand on seeing everything that relates to him directly, or that is being done on his "meter", supports an inference that Gotti is the benefactor paying for the legal representation of others. Because it is fairly clear that the April 18 conversation relates to the civil RICO case in which Santangelo represented others, an inference that Gotti paid Santangelo's fee would advance the government's assertion that Santangelo is "house counsel" to the Gambino Family.

To the extent that a jury may conclude that Santangelo is "house counsel" to the Gambino Family and is answerable to Gotti, the proffered testimony of Gravano and the tape-recorded conversations are immediately probative of one of the elements necessary to the first two counts of the indictment in this case. Thus, Santangelo's relationship to Gotti and to Gotti's associates is properly the object of proof by the government in its case in chief. But, as with Cutler, Shargel, and Pollok, Santangelo cannot present himself as counsel for the defendants when his relationship to those defendants is itself an issue under the consideration of the jury. His presence at counsel table could readily serve as a signal to the jury that the court discounts the government's proof on this point— that the court does not believe this evidence. Moreover, Santangelo could not argue against the existence of the charged RICO enterprise without becoming an unsworn witness.

Disciplinary Rule 5-102(A) reads in pertinent part:

If, after undertaking employment in . . . pending litigation, a lawyer learns or it is obvious that he . . . ought to be called as a witness on behalf of his client, he shall withdraw from . . . the trial . . .

Cross-Motion to Disqualify John Gleeson

Attached to the defendants' Notice of Motion to disqualify John Gleeson is an excerpt from a book, *Mob Star*, co-authored by Jerry Capeci, a columnist for the *New York Daily News*. The excerpted passage describes a 1987 incident from the previous federal criminal trial of John Gotti in this courthouse. That incident was the service of a subpoena on the hospital where Gleeson's wife was employed for the production of her personnel records. Gleeson himself took strong exception to this tactic, and the impropriety of the subpoena was acknowledged by the defense counsel who caused it to be served. Judge Nickerson, in quashing the subpoena on his own motion, remarked that it was "completely off the wall."

Defense counsel in this case now argue that, partially as a result of that incident, Gleeson has an "intense personal interest" in this prosecution and should therefore be disqualified. Upon the most cursory analysis, this argument boils down to the following: 1) An entirely inappropriate subpoena was served for the personnel records of Gleeson's wife; 2) Gleeson (unsurprisingly) took exception to it; 3) the defense attorney responsible recognized its impropriety and apologized in writing; 4) the court quashed the subpoena on its own motion; 5) therefore, Gleeson has an "intense personal interest" in this case warranting his disqualification. The speciousness of this reasoning is so patently apparent as to suggest that the only purpose for asserting it is harassment.

The second basis for the cross-motion is that Gleeson should withdraw withal if it is apparent that he should make himself available as a witness. The argument runs as follows:

1) In an intercepted conversation of November 30, 1989, the following remarks are made:

GOTTI: They hate me . . . prosecutors. If this is f---ing Gleeson again, this f---ing rat mother f---er again. . . .

GRAVANO: You think it's gonna be him?

LOCASCIO: Well, I think them now or later.

GRAVANO: You think it's going to I don't think they're going to be like Gleeson or Giacalone.

2) Gravano decided to cooperate with the government. 3) "It is perfectly reasonable to assume" that Gravano's decision to cooperate was motivated in substantial part by his concern that Gleeson would go to any ends to ensure his conviction, and thereby right the perceived wrongs that the defendants had committed against Gleeson personally. 4) Therefore, Gleeson's involvement in Gravano's decision to cooperate is a proper subject of proof, and Gleeson should be called as a witness.

It should be noted at the outset that it was Gotti, not Gravano, who said the prosecutors hate him. Conceding that Gravano's motive to cooperate may be the subject of cross-examination when Gravano testifies, there is simply no reason why, on the basis of the conversation excerpted above, Gleeson should be available as a witness if it is *Gravano's* motive that the defense believes to be relevant.

There is another cogent reason for concluding that the cross-motion should be denied as baseless. The law is clear, in this circuit and elsewhere, that the defendant can call government counsel as a witness only if required by a compelling and legitimate need. To permit otherwise would be to countenance a procedure which would inevitably confuse the distinction between advocate and witness, between argument and testimony. There is neither a legitimate nor a compelling need—indeed, there is no need at all—for Gleeson to testify.

The third basis for the cross-motion is generated by the unexplained modification of the text of various of the tape recorded [sic] conversations which the government has offered in support of their present motion. Defense counsel is confident that the Court will agree that the reference by the Government to "meter" is not accurate and that what is really said is "on my behalf."

Having listened to the tape recordings in question more than a dozen times, the court finds defendants' confidence misplaced. There is no doubt in the court's mind that the word used by Gotti in the April 18, 1990 conversation is "meter."

The defendants' use of the government's previous draft transcripts in support of their cross-motion is particularly egregious in that it flagrantly violates a prior order of this court. Not long after the defendants were indicted, their counsel requested that the government provide draft transcripts of the intercepted conversations. Upon learning that the government had tentative draft transcripts and was preparing others, the court determined that disclosure would be helpful to the defendants in their preparation for trial. Recognizing that these transcripts were still tentative, and might contain errors, the defendants consented to the entry of an order dated July 1, 1991, which stated in relevant part:

Ordered, that draft transcripts provided prior to trial cannot be used against the government by any person, in any proceeding . . . and it is further

Ordered, that the defendants agree that the use of any draft transcripts will be limited to trial preparation for this case and may not be used at trial by the defendants for any purpose whatsoever. . . .

Because the defense explicitly recognized that the transcripts furnished by the government were tentative and because they consented to the entry of the order set out above, the use of those transcripts here would be more so a fitting object for sanctions than the basis for a successful motion to disqualify a member of the prosecution.

Accordingly, the motion to disqualify Santangelo is granted, and the motion to disqualify Gleeson is denied.

> "There was a parking space in front of
> the restaurant. They pulled into the
> spot. . . . The shooters ran over to them,
> started shooting them."

The Testimony of
an Underboss

*Salvatore Gravano, Gambino family underboss; John
Gleeson, assistant United States attorney*

*Salvatore Gravano served as the underboss in the Gambino fam-
ily under John Gotti. Assistant United States attorney John Gleeson helped prosecute the case of* United States v. John Gotti and
Frank Locascio..

Before United States v. John Gotti and Frank Locascio *opened
in 1992, Gotti's underboss, Salvatore Gravano, signed a plea
agreement with the United States Attorney's Office for the Eastern District of New York. Gravano's defection, which allowed
him to plead guilty to a lesser charge—was a major setback for
the defense. As underboss to Gotti, Gravano had detailed knowledge of the Gambino family's activities, including multiple murders. In his testimony, Gravano describes his and Gotti's involvement in the murder of Gambino family crime boss Paul
Castellano at the end of 1985. The murder of Castellano allowed
Gotti to become the boss of the Gambino family, and eventually,
Gravano to become his underboss.*

Taped Testimony: Salvatore Gravano as questioned by Assistant U.S. Attorney John
Gleeson. Foreword by Ralph Blumenthal and afterword by John Miller, *The Gotti
Tapes: Including the Testimony of Salvatore (Sammy the Bull) Gravano.* New York, NY:
Times Books, 1992, pp. 187–194; pp. 199–205. Copyright © 1992 by Random House,
Inc. Reproduced by permission.

[JohnGleeson, assistant United States attorney] *How long after you pulled into that spot did you see the Lincoln pull up to the right of you?*

[Salvatore Gravano, Gambino family underboss] A couple of minutes.

What did you see?

The Lincoln pulled up with Paul [Castellano, Gambino family crime boss] and Tommy [Bilotti, Paul Castellano's bodyguard] in it.

They pulled up on where, what street were they on?

Right on 42nd Street. They stopped for the light. They had their dome light on. They were talking.

Were they on the street you were parked on?

Right next to us.

You mentioned 42nd Street. You mean—

46th Street.

They were right next to you and John?

Yes.

Did their car have tinted windows?

Yes.

Could you see into their car?

Yes.

Why?

They had the light on. The dome light in the car.

Now, they were on 46th Street facing Third Avenue, correct?

Yes.

Had they yet crossed Third Avenue?

No.

Was the light red or green when they pulled up?

It was red.

Where were you in relation—who was driving that car, by the way?

Tommy.

Where was Paul seated?

In the passenger seat.

In the front passenger?

Yes.

Where was Tommy in relation to you when they pulled up to the light?

He was right next to me. In the next car.

Could you see whether they were doing anything in the car?

They were just talking. I don't know what they were doing.

Okay. So you remember the dome light was on?

Yes.

Okay. Did you look over and see Tommy?

Yes.

At that point did you do anything?

I just turned and I told John they were right next to us. I got on the walkie-talkie and told them that they were stopped at the light, the first car, and they were coming through.

Who did you tell that?

To the people on the other end who were waiting, the shooters and whoever had the walkie-talkie.

Did you know which of those people that were at the scene had the walkie-talkies?

No.

What happened then?

The Hit

The light turned. They pulled up. There was a parking space in front of the restaurant. They pulled into the spot.

The shooters, Tommy got out. The shooters ran over to them, started shooting them.

They watched the surrounding people. We pulled up. I looked at—at Tommy on the floor. I told John he was gone.

We went to Second Avenue, made a right, and went back to my office.

Let's back up a little bit. After they go through the light, where specifically did they park?

Right in front of the restaurant.

From that vantage point, could you see the shooters?

Yes.

What were you watching as this was happening?

The people, the people on the street. The surrounding people.

Why?

Because I was a backup shooter. If anybody would interfere with them, I would come into play.

Did you see who shot who?

No.

Did you see Paul get out of the car?

No.

Did you see Tommy get out of the car?

Yes.

Did you see which one was shot first?

I believe Paul was shot first.

Why?

Tommy squatted down to look through the window, kind of squatted down. And then somebody came up behind him and shot him. He was actually watching Paul get shot.

Did you watch the shooting the whole time it was occurring?

No.

Did you see who shot who?

No.

Later on, did you discuss who actually did the shooting of the four shooters who were on the scene?

Just the four shooters.

Did all of them fire their guns? Did you discuss this later on?

No. We discussed it later on. They didn't all fire their guns. Supposedly, Eddie Lino had reported back that Vinnie Artuso's gun jammed and that he didn't shoot.

You say "supposedly." Who told you this?

John had told me that Eddie Lino reported it back in.

That Vinnie Artuso's gun had jammed?

That Vinnie's gun jammed and he didn't shoot.

Were Bilotti and Castellano shot basically as—right after they parked in front of Sparks Steak House?

Yes.

Did it take a long period of time?

No.

The Getaway

What did you and John Gotti do after the shootings occurred?

We pulled straight up the block.

By that, do you mean straight across Third Avenue and into that block?

Right.

Did you see where the shooters went after the murders took place?

They went straight up the block toward Second Avenue.

You mentioned that you and John Gotti drove through that intersection and into the block on which Sparks is located, correct?

Yes.

Did you drive fast or slow?

Slow.

As you drove past the restaurant, what did you do?

I noticed, I looked down at Tommy Bilotti. I said he was gone. We drove a little faster to go to Second Avenue. We made a right. We went back to my office in Brooklyn.

As you drove past Tommy Bilotti, could you see Castellano?

No.

As you drove down 46th Street—by the way, when you went down 46th Street, did you make a turnoff off 46th Street?

When we hit Second Avenue, we made a turn.

Okay. What kind of a turn?

Right turn on Second Avenue.

Then you testified you drove back to your office on Stillwell Avenue?

Yes, in Brooklyn.

On the way down 46th Street to Second Avenue, did you see any of the shooters?

No.

Did you see them at all after you saw them head down toward Second Avenue after the shooting?

No.

Gotti Becomes Boss

Was there a meeting to appoint a new boss?

Yes, later on Wednesday, a meeting.

Approximately how long after the murders did that take place?

A couple of weeks.

Do you recall where?

It was in Manhattan, lower Manhattan someplace, in a building in a basement.

Do you recall what kind of building it was?

It was a big complex. It was a recreation basement for an entire building. Somebody knew somebody in the building and we had access to this area.

Who came to that meeting?

All the captains.

Anyone else besides all the captains?

A few other people. Angelo, myself, John's brother Genie, Georgie DeCicco, a few other people.

Who presided at that meeting?

Joe Gallo [Gambino family consigliere].

At that point, his role was what?

He was the *consigliere* of the Family and he was in control of the Family.

What happened at the meeting?

They talked a bit. They talked about electing a new boss. I believe Frankie DeCicco [Gambino family capo] got up and nominated John: They went right around the table. Everybody nominated John. John was the boss.

Before the murder of Paul and Tommy, did you have any discussion with Frankie DeCicco as to who would be boss if Paul was killed?

Yes, there were conversations about it.

Can you tell the jury the substance of those conversations that you had with DeCicco?

In the beginning, we were thinking about Frankie DeCicco becoming the boss.

Did he speak to you about that?

Yes.

What did he say?

He said he would be able to be John's underboss, John would not be able to be his underboss, and leave it alone like that.

Did he say—did he tell you anything about what would happen if John was his underboss?

John wouldn't be able to live with it. His ego would bother him and they would clash.

At that time, the time of that meeting when John was appointed boss, what was his position before he was appointed boss?

He was acting captain.

What was Frankie DeCicco's position before he was appointed underboss?

He was a captain.

Was anything done to replace the two of them, once they were elected to boss and underboss?

Yes. Once it was done, John made his underboss, which was Frankie DeCicco. He kept Joe Gallo as his *consigliere*. He replaced Frankie DeCicco with his uncle Georgie DeCicco. And John was replaced by Angelo Ruggiero.

Was that done at the meeting?

That was done at the meeting.

Did there come a point shortly after the meeting when additional captains were made?

About a week after that, I became a captain and Sonny Ciccone became a captain.

Who did you replace?

The old man Toddo.

During the years leading up to your becoming captain, what you just described, could you describe the old man Toddo's activity? Do you understand my question?

No.

He was in charge of a crew?

Yes.

When you replaced him as captain, was that against his wishes?

No, not really.

Why?

He was old. He was tired. He was looking to retire anyway. We had a close relationship. When he was asked to step down, he stepped down gracefully.

Who did Sonny Ciccone replace?

Scotto.

What was Scotto's first name?

Anthony Scotto.

After John Gotti was voted boss by the captains, was there anything else to be done?

We sent out committees again to other Families and notified them that we had elected a new boss, who our new boss was, who our new administration was, and we wanted their approval. For one thing, that we had no sanctions against our Family and we would be able to have no restrictions against our commission seat.

Was there anything you were concerned about in terms of not wanting to have sanctions against the Family?

I don't understand that.

What sanctions might have been imposed as a result of what?

Restrictions, that we couldn't sit and have a vote on the commission.

Were you concerned about why a sanction might be imposed?

Because a boss was killed and there was no explanation of it as yet and we thought there could be a possibility of somebody putting sanctions on us.

Was the approval to have John Gotti on the commission without sanctions sought?

Yes.

How?

We went to each Family and we notified them that we have a boss, we have an administration. We have no problems within our Family. Every captain is in total agreement. We were still investigating the Paul situation, and we didn't want any restrictions on our Family.

Was a response received back? By the way, what other Families were contacted in this regard?

All four Families were contacted.

All four in New York?

Yes.

Was a response received from those four Families?

Yes.

What was the response?

It was a positive response. Every Family sent their blessings and they accepted it. Except for the Genovese Family. They accepted it but they told "Joe Piney" [nickname of Joseph Armone, Gambino family consigliere serving a prison sentence] that to the exception, there was a rule broken, someday somebody would have to answer for that if and when the commission ever got together again.

And by that, what did you understand them to be referring to?

The rule with a boss being killed.

Did there ever come a point when the administration of the Gambino Family had to answer for breaking that rule?

No.

After John became the boss, Mr. Gravano, as far as you knew, did the rest of the Gambino Family, did the captains, know who had killed Paul and Tommy?

We never told them.

That wasn't my question. You became part of the administration, correct?

Yes.

As part of the administration, did you have regular contact with other people in the Family?

Yes.

Did the other people include the captains?

Yes.

Did you speak to them from time to time about the prior administration?

Yes.

Did you speak about Paul Castellano?

Yes, we did.

You mentioned that there was unhappiness within the Family before the murder of Paul?

Yes.

Was that unhappiness discussed from time to time?

Occasionally.

After the murder, did you ever admit directly to anybody else in the Family that you had been involved in the murder of Paul Castellano?

No.

Why not?

Because of that rule, we would never talk about it or admit.

> "Gravano with a gun was a dangerous
> man, no doubt about it. But Gravano's
> mouth would prove just as lethal."

Convicting a Crime Boss

John Miller

*John Miller is currently the assistant director of public affairs for
the Federal Bureau of Investigation (FBI).*

*After attempting, but failing, to convict crime boss John Gotti
three times, federal prosecutors convinced Salvatore Gravano to
testify against him. The defection of an underboss (second in
command) surprised many: Organized crime no longer seemed
to have the power to command loyalty. John Miller explains that
because Gravano was so important to the federal case against
Gotti, the Federal Bureau of Investigation (FBI) worked hard to
keep him happy and to keep him safe. Even in the courtroom,
numerous FBI agents formed a barrier between organized crime
figures in the audience and Gravano. Prosecutors knew, however,
that Gravano's testimony would only help their case against
Gotti if he remained consistent on the witness stand. Adding to
the tension of the courtroom drama, a number of people at-
tended the trial who believed that Gravano had played a role in
the death of a family member. In the end, Gravano remained
steadfast on the witness stand, providing incriminating evidence
that would help convict Gotti in 1992.*

John Miller, *The Gotti Tapes: Including the Testimony of Salvatore (Sammy the Bull)
Gravano*, New York, NY: Times Books, 1992, pp. 368–377. Afterword copyright ©
1992 by John Miller Enterprises. Reproduced by permission.

It was Monday, March 2, 1992, when Salvatore (Sammy the Bull) Gravano first sang for his supper, and the government wasn't taking any chances with the highest-ranking, most significant mobster ever to rat on his gang in U.S. history.

Security that day was even tighter than usual. A crowd of deputy U.S. marshals was packed into the rows of spectators. A line of muscle-bound FBI agents—the special Hostage Rescue Team sent up to New York from the FBI academy in Quantico, Virginia—sat along a bench just inside the well of the courtroom. Sporting unfashionable crew cuts, they were the Bureau's shooters, commandos in gray suits, the meanest dudes the Bureau had. Directly behind them sat eleven of John Gotti's closest pals and supporters. They didn't seem pleased to have their view of the proceedings blocked by the wall of G-men in front of them. The feds, for their part, didn't seem to mind at all.

The tension was palpable. Gravano's appearance was the break the government needed and the defense had feared. For Gravano was the last man John Gotti had expected to betray him. He loved Sammy. And Sammy, he felt sure, loved him. Never before had Gravano refused an order. In the past, when Gotti had barked, Sammy bit. He was a tough guy's tough guy. That he might turn rabid and attack his master was a possibility Gotti apparently had never reckoned on.

Why Gotti never saw it coming remains a mystery. After all, Gravano's entire history suggested that when backed into a corner, he always took the most drastic way out. That usually meant whacking whoever he regarded as standing in his way. His reputation as one of the more feared enforcers in the Mafia was well deserved. He was a guy who never seemed to lose even a nanosecond's worth of sleep no matter whom he killed—whether the victim happened to be his wife's brother or a business partner or his best friend. Once it became clear that Gravano had decided to rat on Gotti, the Gambino clan sought to dismiss his bloody deeds as the work of a man who didn't really have the balls to pull the trigger himself. As one of Gotti's friends put it: "Sammy was a drugstore cowboy. He had a fancy hat, he wore nice shiny boots, but he didn't know how to ride a horse. He didn't kill nobody. He'd get two kids to kill them. Then a few weeks later, he'd get someone to kill the two kids." But this was a distinction without much difference. Certainly it mattered not at all to the nineteen dead men whose murders Gravano would confess to.

The Government's Key Witness

Gravano with a gun was a dangerous man, no doubt about it. But Gravano's mouth would prove just as lethal. The government had taken steps to ensure that Gravano wouldn't crack once he took the stand. The moment he had decided to switch sides, his care and feeding became a top priority for the FBI. He was removed from New York's Metropolitan Correctional Center, where Gotti and his codefendant Frank Locascio were held, and flown secretly to Quantico. The Bureau went to great lengths to keep Gravano happy. Even his passion for boxing was indulged. A host of young agents volunteered to get into the ring with Sammy, never doubting that they would easily beat this rank amateur. They were wrong. It quickly became a matter of pride. The Bureau flew in a big Indian agent from Illinois who had a reputation with his hands. He slammed Gravano with a body punch that caused Sammy to growl and double over, holding his sides. For a moment, his government minders were scared. What if things got out of hand? What if Gravano were injured so badly that his testimony was delayed? "Jesus," one agent laughed, "what if he got f---ing amnesia?" They slacked off on the sparring after that.

The government couldn't afford to lose this case. Gotti had already beaten them three times before. The FBI's image was at stake. If Gravano was going to help them tie the bow, they would find a way to make sure the knot would be pulled tight. Gravano would help them get Gotti in exchange for a maximum twenty years in the pen, and in the process the Gambino Family would be gutted. Gravano was a gusher, and his decision to tell them everything he knew was black gold. His memory would prove nearly photographic. No detail from his violent past was too small or too gory to have been forgotten. Best of all, Sammy told them everything about the Paul Castellano[former Gambino family boss] hit—how it was planned, who the designated shooters were, how it went down.

Still, the government couldn't be entirely sure that Gravano wouldn't buckle under pressure. He was, they realized, all alone. His wife, Debra, and his son and daughter had vowed never to have anything to do with him again. As far as they were concerned, he was history. They had refused to accompany him into the Federal Witness Protection Program. He would be left to twist in the wind with his newfound friends.

Gravano, the "Rising Star"

"Our next witness is Salvatore Gravano," said John Gleeson, the assistant U.S. attorney.

"Okay," said Judge I. Leo Glasser.

The courtroom on the fourth floor of the Brooklyn Federal Courthouse was utterly silent. Nobody moved. Even Gotti, whose constant gestures of contempt had driven the prosecutors nuts, sat still. Only the smirk that was perpetually stuck on his mug seemed to twitch. It took an agonizing four full minutes from the time Gleeson called Gravano as a witness until the door behind the witness stand opened. Suddenly Sammy entered, surrounded by agents in front and behind him. No one spoke or coughed or even seemed to breathe. I remembered the first time I ever saw this man they called The Bull.

As the principal investigative reporter for WNBC-TV, I had been assigned to keep track of John Gotti as he rose to the top of what was regarded as America's largest Cosa Nostra Family. No one had ever gotten an interview with Gotti, and in late October 1987, I was determined to be the first, even if I had to "ambush" him with his henchmen as he took one of his frequent "walk talks" outside the Ravenite Social Club, his hangout in Little Italy. My camera crews took up their positions. I knew from past experience that the men who always accompanied Gotti would try to cover the lenses of any nosy cameras that managed to come too close. On this particular night, though, I had come prepared with more cameras and lights than Gotti's men had hands.

As Gotti and two men neared the middle of the block, I struck. He tried to escape. The two men accompanying him, one tall and the other short, tried their best, cursing and shoving my crew. But one of the three cameras we had was always in Gotti's face as I peppered him with questions I knew he was never going to answer like "Are you the head of the Gambino Crime Family?"

"Easy, Sammy," he said to the short one.

"Frank!" he called to the taller man as he wagged an index finger. Gotti was a man who, above all things, was obsessed with appearances. He professed bewilderment: "I always treat you like a gentleman, John. This is no good." But it was good enough to make the evening news, and that was good enough for me.

Later, I showed the videotape to the late John Gurnee, perhaps the New York City detective with the most intimate knowledge of Gotti and his men. "Who are these other two guys with John?" I asked. "The tall guy is Frankie Locascio, an old-time wiseguy," he said. "The little guy is Sammy the Bull. He's the guy to watch. A rising star."

Gravano Takes the Stand

Now, five years later, Gravano was a star all right—the government's, and now I and everyone else would get a chance to watch Sammy give the performance of his life. Like everyone else, I wondered how he would do on the stand. Would he freeze up? Or back out? Would he hold up on cross-examination?

Gleeson, who had been taunted by Gotti as a "meek little mouse," stood at the lectern at the far end of the jury box Gravano, his hair greased back, and decked out in a gray double-breasted suit, took his seat in the witness box at the other end. The tall, thin Ivy League prosecutor with the horn-rimmed glasses couldn't have provided a starker contrast. The questioning began. Sammy's answers, delivered in a calm and icy monotone, would prove so compelling in their brutal candor and detail as to strip Gotti and Locascio's lawyers of any convincing defense.

The defense team was stunned, deprived of any viable strategy capable of undoing the damage that was daily being inflicted on their clients. Albert Krieger, Gotti's lawyer, was said to be a fearsome cross-examiner. A man with a rich baritone and a shaved head, he looked like a cross between Kojak and Daddy Warbucks. Anthony Cardinale, Locascio's attorney, had grown up in Brooklyn and had become partners with F. Lee Bailey before striking out on his own. During the cross-examination, Gravano refused to be rattled. Nothing seemed to work. Not the courtly manner of Krieger, who was at pains to offend neither the judge nor the jury. Not the brasher tactics of Cardinale, who became increasingly exasperated with the judge's refusal to allow seven of the eight witnesses the defense wanted to call, including an audio expert to question the content and meaning of the tape transcripts that had been so meticulously prepared by the FBI.

Cardinale went ballistic. If the government was permitted to put a witness on the stand to testify as to the accuracy of the FBI's transcripts, why couldn't the defense put on a witness to give its interpretation? "I can't understand it," said Cardinale, "and I'm sorry if I'm losing my temper. I have had enough . . . I can't believe what's going on here. I can't believe it, as a practicing lawyer for fifteen years in cases as complex as this—"

Judge Glasser cut Cardinale off: "I'm holding you, sir, in summary contempt, and I'll prepare a certificate to that effect in accordance with 42(a) of the Federal Rules of Criminal Procedure. I'll deal with the penalty imposed, Mr. Cardinale—"

Cardinale interrupted the judge in mid-sentence: "Do it right now, judge, really."

At the defense table, Krieger turned pale. Gotti, however, looked elated. When the yelling was over and Cardinale had returned to the defense table, Gotti reached over to shake his hand. Krieger, for his part, sought to placate the judge by blaming Cardinale's outburst on pressure and stress. Gotti would give Krieger hell for it later.

Confronting Gravano

The differences in style between the defense attorneys were obvious to even the most casual of observers. Where Krieger was careful and conservative, Cardinale was cocky and aggressive. Both men, however, seemed baffled by the government's case. Only John Gotti seemed to know where he was going. And all he seemed to want was a good fight—with the judge, the prosecutor, and, most of all, with his ex-best friend, Sammy the Bull.

Gotti wasn't the only one who wanted to confront Gravano. During Sammy's second day on the stand, a woman screaming in Italian tried to burst through the courtroom doors. United States Marshal Charles Healey had his security officers pull the distraught woman into his office. Healey, a retired homicide detective with a soft bedside manner, gave her a tissue and asked her to explain herself. Her name, she said, was Anna Carini, and she was the mother of two sons who had gone to see Sammy Gravano one warm night in 1986. That was the last time she had seen them alive.

I remembered the Carini brothers quite vividly. I was there when the cops pulled their bullet-ridden bodies out of two cars that had been parked together. They both wore fancy warm-up suits. One had a weight lifter's belt around his waist. That they had been dealing drugs, robbing banks, and doing small-time hits for a local hood was an open neighborhood secret. Apparently only their mother didn't know. She did know one thing, however: somehow, Sammy Gravano was to blame.

The following day a woman named Rose Massa broke free from the long line of would-be spectators who waited sometimes all day and in vain to get into the trial. As she approached me, I could see she was nervous and upset. She quickly introduced herself and got to the point. Her brother was Michael DeBatt. He had been killed in the summer of 1987, in Tali's, the club Gravano owned in Brooklyn. Sammy had come to the funeral. Indeed, there was hardly a funeral of any of his victims that he missed. Rose Massa had been Gravano's secretary at the construction company he headed. She told me she wanted to see Sammy on the stand, but the marshals had refused to let her up. I spoke to Healey, and he agreed to make room for her provided she promised not to make a scene. She took a seat in the back of the courtroom, and left at the lunch break, telling me, with a shake of her head, "In our neighborhood, Sammy's middle name was 'Do the Right Thing,' and now look at him."

Each day Gravano was on the stand a young man in a turtle-neck sat in the second row. He stared at Gravano day after day. Joey D'Angelo was just nineteen. Years before, Joey's father, Stymie, had been killed in a stick-up in Tali's. He told me Gravano thought of him as an adopted son. D'Angelo was a tough kid, saying he had met Gravano "at the funeral parlor after my father died." Ever since, he had worshiped the man.

Joey learned from Gravano that the key to being a man was to do the right thing and keep your mouth shut. I asked him what he saw in Gravano's eyes when he caught his glance on the witness stand. "I saw shame," he replied.

An Anonymous Jury

After Gravano had been on the stand for five days straight, Judge Glasser suspended the trial for a day so that a member of the jury could attend a family funeral. The jury was anonymous and sequestered. Marshals guarded the twelve jurors and four alternates around the clock. Forty hotel rooms at the rate of $106 a night were rented. Limousines with dark tinted windows took them to and from hotels. Their names were kept secret from both the defense and prosecution. Not even the judge was permitted to know their names. The list was locked in the court clerk's safe, and only a court order could break it out.

Concern for the jury's safety was to be expected. Despite the fact that the jury in Gotti's last trial had been anonymous, it was not sequestered. One of the jurors, it turned out, was friendly with one of Gotti's friends. Prosecutors said the man made a deal to sell his vote for $60,000, and on February 24, 1992, smack in the middle of Gotti's new trial, the man was arrested and charged with obstruction of justice. He pleaded not guilty. The government was determined that this time things would be different. This time they were.

Convicting Gotti

After Sammy's testimony, the trial was, for all practical purposes, over. As far as the government was concerned, Gravano had done his finest piece of work, and it began to look as if Gotti was finally finished. The defense took a last, desperate shot at Gravano and the government in their closing statements. For two days, Krieger and Cardinale railed against the prosecutors, accusing them of putting on a show trial and cutting a deal with a ruthless killer who would do anything to save his own skin.

The jury didn't buy it. On April 2, after deliberating for only a day and a half, the panel of seven women and five men put an end to the reign of the most feared gangster in decades. John Gotti showed no emotion as the forewoman pronounced him guilty of all fourteen counts, ranging from murder to racketeering to tax evasion, with which he had been charged. (Although Frank Locascio was acquitted of one minor charge of illegal gambling, he too went down for the count.) Ever the boss, ever the fighter, Gotti patted his lawyers on the back and promised his demoralized supporters that he'd win on appeal. "We'll be all right," Gotti said as the marshals led him from the courtroom and back to the Manhattan jail cell to contemplate the several life terms and the few hundred years behind bars that he now faced.

The government was jubilant. "The Teflon is gone," said the head of the FBI's New York office. "The Don is covered with Velcro."

Outside her parents' home in Howard Beach, Queens, Gotti's daughter Victoria was defiant, telling reporters that the whole trial was a sham. "My father," she said, her voice proud and strong, "is the last of the Mohicans."

Organizations to Contact

The editors have compiled the following list of organizations concerned with the issues debated in this book. The descriptions are derived from materials provided by the organizations. All have publications or information available for interested readers. The list was compiled on the date of publication of the present volume; the information provided here may change. Be aware that many organizations take several weeks or longer to respond to inquiries, so allow as much time as possible.

American Civil Liberties Union (ACLU)
125 Broad Street, 18th Floor, New York, NY   10004
(212) 549-2500 • fax: (212) 549-2646
e-mail: aclu@aclu.org
Web site: www.aclu.org

The American Civil Liberties Union (ACLU) is a national organization that defends Americans' civil rights as guaranteed in the U.S. Constitution. It advocates for freedom of all forms of speech, including pornography, flag-burning, and political protest. The ACLU offers numerous reports, fact sheets, and policy statements on free speech issues, which are available on its Web site. Some of these publications include "Free Speech Under Fire," "Freedom of Expression," and, for students, "Ask Sybil Liberty About Your Right to Free Expression."

American Judicature Society
The Opperman Center at Drake University
Des Moines, IA   50311
(800) 626-4089 • fax: (515) 279-3090
Web site: www.ajs.org

The American Judicature Society is made up of lawyers, judges, law teachers, and government officials who promote effective justice and combat court delays. The society conducts research, offers a consulting service, and publishes the magazine *Judicature*.

Brennan Center for Justice at NYU School of Law
161 Avenue of the Americas, 12th Floor
New York, NY   10013
(212) 998-6733 • fax: (212) 995-4550
Web site: www.fepproject.org

The Brennan Center for Justice is a nonpartisan public policy and law institute that focuses on the fundamental issues of democracy and justice. The Brennan Center for Justice's work ranges from voting rights to redistricting reform, from access to the courts to presidential power in the fight against terrorism. The Brennan Center combines scholarship, legislative and legal advocacy, and communications to win meaningful, measurable change in the public sector.

Cato Institute
1000 Massachusetts Avenue NW, Washington, DC   20001
(202) 842-0200 • fax: (202) 842-3490
Web site: www.cato.org

The Cato Institute is a libertarian public-policy research foundation. It evaluates government policies and offers reform proposals and commentary on its Web site. Its publications include the *Cato Policy Analysis* series of reports, which have covered topics such as "Fighting Back: Crime, Self-Defense, and the Right to Carry a Handgun" and "Trust the People: The Case Against Gun Control." It also publishes the magazine *Regulation*, the *Cato Policy Report*, and books such as *The Samurai, The Mountie,* and *The Cowboy: Should America Adopt the Gun Controls of Other Democracies?*

First Amendment Center at Vanderbilt University
1207 Eighteenth Avenue South, Nashville, TN   37212
(615) 727-1600 • fax: (615) 727-1319
e-mail: info@fac.org
Web site: www.firstamendmentcenter.org

The First Amendment Center works to preserve and protect First Amendment freedoms through information and education. The center serves as a forum for the study and exploration of free-expression issues, including freedom of speech, of the press, and of religion, and the rights to assemble and to petition the government.

International Association for the Study of Organized Crime (IASOC)
Department of Criminal Justice, Bloomington, IN   47405
(812) 855-0899
e-mail: iasoc_office@yahoo.com
Web site: www.iasoc.net

The International Association for the Study of Organized Crime (IASOC) is a program at Indiana University that studies organized crime efforts and publishes many papers and briefings on the subject.

Milton S. Eisenhower Foundation
1875 Connecticut Avenue NW, Washington, DC   20009
(202) 234-8104
e-mail: info@eisenhowerfoundation.org
Web site: www.eisenhowerfoundation.org

The Milton S. Eisenhower Foundation consists of individuals dedicated to reducing crime in inner-city neighborhoods through community programs. It believes that more federally funded programs such as Head Start and Job Corps will improve education and job opportunities for youths, thus reducing juvenile crime and violence. The foundation's publications include the report *To Establish Justice, To Insure Domestic Tranquility: A Thirty-Year Update of the National Commission on the Causes and Prevention of Violence* and the book *Youth Investment and Police Mentoring.*

International Association of Chiefs of Police (IACP)
515 N. Washington Street, Alexandria, VA   22314
(703) 836-6767
Web site: www.theiacp.org

The goals of the International Association of Chiefs of Police (IACP) are to advance the science and art of police services. IACP helped create the FBI Identification Division and the

Uniform Crime Records system and also spearheaded the national use of fingerprint identification. It publishes *Police Chief* magazine and reports on various law enforcement policies, policing trends, and legislative issues.

National Institute of Justice (NIJ)

Box 6000, Rockville, MD   20849
(301) 519-3420
Web site: www.ncjrs.org

A component of the Office of Justice Programs of the U.S. Department of Justice, the National Institute of Justice (NIJ) supports research on crime, criminal behavior, and crime prevention. The National Criminal Justice Reference Service (NCJRS) acts as a clearinghouse that provides information and research about criminal justice. Its publications include the research briefs "Reducing Youth Gun Violence: An Overview of Programs and Initiatives," "Impacts of the 1994 Assault Weapons Ban," and "Homicide in Eight U.S. Cities: Trends, Context, and Policy Implications."

U.S. Department of Justice

Office of Justice Programs, Washington, DC   20530-0001
(202) 514-2000
Web sites: www.usdoj.gov

The U.S. Department of Justice protects citizens by maintaining effective law enforcement, crime prevention, crime detection, and prosecution and rehabilitation of offenders. Through its Office of Justice Programs, the department operates the National Institute of Justice, the Office of Juvenile Justice and Delinquency Prevention, and the Bureau of Justice Statistics. Its publications include fact sheets, research packets, bibliographies, and the semiannual journal *Juvenile Justice.*

Victims of Crime and Leniency (VOCAL)

PO Box 4449, Montgomery, AL   36103
(334) 262-7197 • fax: (334) 262-7197

Victims of Crime and Leniency (VOCAL) seeks to ensure that a crime victim's rights are recognized and protected. It believes the U.S. justice system goes to great lengths to protect the rights of criminals while discounting those of the victim. VOCAL has been responsible for introducing or supporting fourteen victim's rights bills, including the Victim's Bill of Rights which guarantees that victims will be notified prior to the release of prisoners convicted of crimes perpetrated against them. It publishes the quarterly newsletter *VOCAL Voice*.

For Further Research

Books

Howard Abadinsky, *Organized Crime*. 8th ed. Florence, KY: Wadsworth, 2006.

Shana Alexander, *The Pizza Connection: Lawyers, Money, Drugs, Mafia*. New York: Weidenfeld & Nicolson, 1988.

Herman Benson, *Rebels, Reformers and Racketeers: How Insurgents Transformed the Labor Movement*. Bloomington, IN: Authorhouse, 2004.

Howard Blum, *Gangland: How the FBI Broke Up the Mob*. New York: Simon and Schuster, 1993.

Ralph Blumenthal, *Last Days of the Sicilians: At War with the Mafia: The FBI Assault on the Pizza Connection*. New York: Random House, 1988.

Joe Bonanno, *Man of Honor*. New York: Simon and Schuster, 1983.

Kenneth C. Crowe, *Collision: How the Rank and File Took Back the Teamsters*. New York: Scribner's and Sons, 1992.

Douglas Feiden, *Sleeping the Good Sleep: The Life and Times of John Gotti*. New York: Random House, 1990.

Stephen Fox, *Blood and Power: Organized Crime in Twentieth-Century America*. New York: Morrow, 1989.

Stanislaw Frankowski, *Preventive Detention: A Comparative and International Law Perspective*. New York: Springer, 1992.

Michael J. Harper, Samuel Estreicher, and Joan Flynn, *Labor Law: Cases, Materials and Problems*. 6th ed. New York: Aspen, 2007.

Robert J. Kelly, *The Upperworld and the Underworld: Case Studies of Racketeering and Business Infiltrations in the United States.* New York: Springer, 1999.

Paul Lunde, *Organized Crime: An Inside Guide to the World's Most Successful Industry.* New York: DK, 2006.

Michael D. Lyman, *Gangland: Drug Trafficking by Organized Criminals.* Springfield, IL: Thomas, 1989.

Mafia: The Government's Secret File on Organized Crime. New York: Collins, 2007.

Joseph Pistone with Richard Woodley, *Donnie Brasco: My Undercover Life in the Mafia.* New York: American Library, 1988.

Thomas Reppetto, *Bringing Down the Mob: The War Against the American Mafia.* New York: Henry Holt, 2006.

Patrick Ryan and George E. Rush, *Understanding Organized Crime in Global Perspective: A Reader.* London: Sage, 1997.

Periodicals

General Articles

G. Robert Blakey, "Law and the Continuing Enterprise: Perspectives on RICO," *Notre Dame Law Review*, vol. 65, 1990, pp. 873–1105.

———and B. Gettings, "RICO: Evening Up the Odds," *Trial*, October 1980, pp. 1658–1660.

Teresa Carpenter, "The Mob Within the Mob," *New York Times*, September 11, 1988.

Murray Kempton, "Knowing RICO's Foibles," *Newsday*, March 22, 1987.

Ed Magnuson, "Hard Days for the Mafia: The Feds Turn the Screws," *Time*, March 4, 1985.

Chapter One: *United States v. Local 560* (1984)

Business Week, "A New Weapon Against Labor Racketeers," February 14, 1983.

Michael Hoyt, "Hostile Takeovers: The Mob Ran Teamsters Local 560 for Decades, Until the Government Grabbed Control," *Mother Jones*, December 1988.

Eugene Kiely, "Local 560: Proof Is in the Vote; Election Is Test of U.S. Efforts to Clean Up Teamsters," *Record*, November 27, 1988.

Craig Mello, "Operating on Sick Unions," *Across the Board*, March 1988.

Eugene H. Methvin, "The Liberation of the Teamsters," *National Review*, March 30, 1992.

Elliot Pinsley, "Introducing Democracy to Teamsters Local 560," *Record*, November 1, 1987.

Time, "Teamster Shuffle," December 19, 1988.

Rich Wilner, "Apparel Trucker Charged in Union Busting," *Daily News Record*, October 14, 1988.

Chapter Two: *United States v. Badalamenti* (1986)

Jacob V. Lamar Jr., "Family Affairs: Two Mafia Cases Go to Court," *Time*, October 14, 1985.

Arnold H. Lubasch, "Drug Defendant Reticent on Mafia Past," *New York Times*, October 19, 1986.

Michael Massing, "The Pizza Connection: Lawyers, Money, Drugs, Mafia," *New York Review of Books*, March 30, 1989.

Jim Miller, "The Pizza Connection," *Newsweek*, August 29, 1988.

Time, "Extra Cheese: Busting a Pizza Connection," April 23, 1984.

Time, "Pizza Penance: A Jury Convicts 18 Mobsters," March 16, 1987.

U.S. News & World Report, "Breaking the 'Pizza Connection,'" April 23, 1984.

Mary Vespa, "The Pizza Connections," *People Weekly*, September 5, 1988.

Chapter Three: *United States v. Salerno* (1987)

Charles Krauthammer, "The Miranda Scandal; Judicial Activism, Meese Style," *Washington Post*, January 30, 1987.

Marian E. Lupo, "*United States v. Salerno*: 'A Loaded Weapon Ready for the Hand,'" *Brooklyn Law Review*, Spring 1988.

Curtis J. Sitomer, "Court Limits Bail Right," *Christian Science Monitor*, May 27, 1987.

Curtis J. Sitomer, "Jail Without Bail," *Christian Science Monitor*, January 22, 1987.

Michael W. Youtt, "The Effect of *Salerno v. United States* on the Use of State Preventative Detention Legislation: A New Definition of Due Process," *Georgia Law Review*, Spring 1988.

Chapter Four: *United States v. John Gotti and Frank Locascio* (1992)

Howard Blum, "How the FEDS Got Gotti," *New York*, November 1, 1993.

Joe Collins, "A Matter of Honor: One Cop's Lifelong Pursuit of John Gotti and the Mob," *Booklist*, September 1, 1993.

Frederic Dannen, "Defending the Mafia," *New Yorker*, February 21, 1994.

Bill Hewitt, "Bad Fellas," *People Weekly*, March 23, 1992.

Sharon LaFraniere, "Hurt by Convictions, Mafia Still a Target; On Eve of Gotti Trial, Some See Mob's Demise Within a Decade," *Washington Post*, January 20, 1992.

Gene Lyons, "Gangland: How the FBI Broke the Mob," *Entertainment Weekly*, November 5, 1993.

Peter Maas, "Cosa Nostra's Yellow Ribbons," *Esquire*, October 1992.

Michael Massing, "The Gotti Tapes: Including the Testimony of Salvatore (Sammy the Bull) Gravano," *New York Review of Books*, December 3, 1992.

Joe Treen, "Lessons in Time," *People Weekly*, August 10, 1992.

Index